UNDERSTANDING THE SKYDIVE

Understanding
the
Skydive

BY
ERIK JOHNSON

1st edition
LAMPLIGHTER PRESS
ROME, GEORGIA

LCCN: 2002090003
ISBN 0-9717430-0-2
Printed in the United States of America

Dedicated to Michelle

Contents

Introduction

A skydive is a departure from an aircraft in flight, for the purpose of recreation or competition, while using a parachute for all or part of the subsequent descent. A skydiver skydives. But the story doesn't end here. Who skydives, how the life cycle of a skydive develops, and why one would want to skydive are all legitimate questions.

Some approaches to skydiving have proven to work better than others and have had a long term effect on the who, what, where, how and why human beings leave the familiarity of an airplane for the bareness of the earth's atmosphere. The goal of this book is to explain some of these approaches, ideas, and the cultural forces driving the practical exercises learned in formal parachute training. Even though the book contains how-to aspects, it is not a how-to-skydive book. Specific equipment and training conditions always vary. Learning to skydive takes practice under the watchful eye of someone who knows both how to skydive and how to teach skydiving. That person is a rated skydiving instructor.

People start jumping from planes for many reasons. While most have an exhilarating first experience, a majority choose not to complete formal training. For those who do continue, skydiving evolves from an isolated experience on life's landscape into a sport, recreation, or social outlet. As a sport, skydiving provides kinesthetic and social opportunities within a colorful, exciting environment. As recreation it is an outlet for healthful entertainment. Skydivers find a sense of personal fulfillment within the sport, recreation, or avocation's uniquely challenging environment.

In recent years the numbers of people making skydives and the numbers of skydives they make have mushroomed.

Each year around 300,000 people representing almost every demographic take to the skies to make over three million jumps at 300 parachute centers, or drop zones, scattered around the United States. Through this exposure the collective practice of skydiving has matured.

These skydiver's collective experiences pervade every nook of the sport's colorful spectrum. At one end are skydivers making a first training jump. In the middle are licensed skydivers pursuing a range of interests (disciplines). These interests range from making a few jumps a month with friends to jumping with a camera to jumping competitively. At the other end of the skydiver spectrum are leaders on the "cutting edge" of innovation, exploration, and performance. This group helps define skydiving's range of possibilities and pass what they find back down to the mainstream.

The interests skydivers cultivate as they mature grows to a large degree from where they skydive. Every parachute center, or drop zone, is unique, and like a family helps to build frames of reference for safety, performance, interests, and skydiving culture. Selection of an initial drop zone, for example, helps decide which mode of training is pursued and how that mode is administered.

Our definition, "departure of an aircraft in flight," might lead one to believe that a skydive begins when a skydiver leaves an airplane and ends with a successful landing. In practice, the skydive begins well before boarding said aircraft and doesn't end until well after landing under that parachute. What happens between the idea and its resolution is the skydive. But what happens between that idea and its resolution? Why would an intelligent, rational human being throw his or herself from the apparent safety of a functioning airplane? These questions are the focus of this book and are areas ripe for discussion. Let's begin our exploration of this ethereal scene painted on an abstract canvas with a look at who is skydiving, where they are doing it, and how.

A Skydiver By Any Other Name...

Skydivers are a varied breed. While each person is unique, skydivers as a group have interested scientists for years. In 1969, Fenz and Epstein compared physiological responses in skydiving and skydiving related activities. What they found were differences in anxiety peaks. As skydivers in this study gained experience, their height of excitement moved from the airplane door opening to just before arriving at the airport. In Fenz and Epstein's interpretation, "experienced" skydivers (defined as those with over 100 jumps) learned to control or repress anxiety to a more adaptive time when it did not overwhelm them.

In another study, John Delk examined experienced skydivers and found, collectively, that they are "more intelligent and have more formal education than the general population." Delk used the Minnesota Multiphasic Personality Inventory (MMPI) to assess group personality traits. Results indicated that skydivers are more "free of anxiety, more open, more impulsive, and more frequently reject traditional religious tenets" than do members of the general population. According to Delk, skydivers are also more self confident, extroverted, and free of health worries.

In 1990 Stephen Lang developed a model for voluntary risk taking using skydivers. Lang, unlike Delk and Fenz, developed his framework while actively involved in the sport. He labeled voluntary risk takers "edgeworkers" and described their drive to skydive as "an approach to the boundary between order and disorder, form and formlessness." Mastery of individual skills and a striving for self actualizing experiences help characterize edgeworkers. In fact, according to Lang, it is this sense of control, real or imagined, that separates edgeworkers from thrill seekers or gamblers. Common throughout Lang's study was a belief in skill, control, flexibility, and a "mergence of the individual with the activity."

Only a small portion of skydiving actually takes place in the air. By far the majority of drop zone time is spent deciding what to do in the air, figuring out how to do it, preparing for it, discussing it after it's over, and preparing to do it again. And when the airplanes are tied down it is time to get to know the people who have been around the drop zone during the day. Some of them are instructors, photographers, or other staff responsible for keeping the facility operating. But most are recreational skydivers from wide ranging backgrounds; each with a story.

Drop zone activities create a sense of community. There are numerous opportunities for social interaction. Skydivers often play games or cook out and have bonfires to promote conversation. All these functions, spontaneous or planned, bring people closer together, promote enthusiasm, and most important, help to educate and assimilate new skydivers.

There is little doubt that skydiving attracts a certain type of personality, and once attracted reinforces or activates some predispositions. People may skydive for the almost sexual buildup and release it provides. Some skydive to experience a sense of control or mastery they otherwise feel lacking in their life. They may skydive to be part of a group of vital, interesting, and diverse people.

To keep these independent edgeworkers jumping out of airplanes a whole troupe of actors team up to form a parachute center's engine. Student skydivers, teams, organizers, and instructors are needed on the drop zone. Pilots, parachute riggers, photographers, manifestors, aircraft maintenance people, and a manager are also needed. The larger the drop zone the more staff is needed to keep activities cued, airplanes flying, and people jumping.

SECTION I

THE ACTORS

The classification of skydivers

Skydivers are classified by experience and how frequently they jump. Frequency, or currency, is relative and defined by who you ask. Experience is defined as a total number of jumps, numbers of jumps in a specific discipline, or amount of time in the sport.

"Students," skydivers without a license, must meet more stringent currency requirements than licensed skydivers. Students need to be immersed in the learning environment as frequently as possible to develop safe behavior patterns early in the skydiving career. Parachute use lies at the core of this skydiver training. Learning how to operate parachute equipment, being able to read winds, pick a suitable exit point, track, land, and react to an array of situational challenges is part of being a skydiver. It is important that student skydivers build as much of this survival experience as possible while under competent supervision so that the most effective skills develop.

After obtaining a license the "student" becomes a "recreational skydiver." Obtaining a license gives the newcomer an opportunity to try out personalized modes of aerial expression.

Student- any skydiver not holding a license

A License- Recognizes novice skydivers and certifies that holders are able to pack their own main parachute, and jump without direct supervision.

B License- Recognizes intermediate skydivers and certifies that holders may make night jumps, formation jumps, and participate in record attempts.

C License- Recognizes advanced skydivers and certifies that holders may coach other licensed skydivers (after obtaining an appropriate rating), and may participate in some formal competitions.

D License- Recognizes master skydivers and certifies that holders may participate in all USPA competitions, are eligible for all USPA ratings, and may be appointed Safety and Training Advisor.

"Professional skydiver" is a broad category catching almost anyone working in the industry. It includes the instructor, parachute rigger, coach, or organizer. Many duties on a drop zone require these people and their skills. Someone must manage advertising, scheduling, and maintenance. Someone has to collect money and record which skydivers are on which airplane. Someone has to train and supervise students. Someone has to fly the airplane. Someone has to organize recreational skydivers. Someone has to pack parachutes. Someone has to sell equipment. Professional skydivers carry out these responsibilities.

The Drop Zone

The Care and Feeding of a Drop Zone

Drop zone operators manage a parachute center's staff and the physical facilities making up the center. A center is composed first, of people, and second of buildings, aircraft, and concessions. A "building" may be as simple as a tarp to keep the sun off or as complex as multiple, specialized hangers, shops, and offices. Aircraft run the gamut from single engine, three-jumper, Cessna-172s to multiple, 20 or 30 jumper multi-engine airplanes.

To start a drop zone one only needs an airplane, an airfield, and a few skydivers with equipment. Soon, more skydivers arrive and there is work to do. Someone has to remove trash, keep records, and maintain the airplane. Eventually someone's brother wants to learn and an instructor is needed.

Student training equipment and a staff of instructors are a must for any level of student training. Every parachute system that a student uses must be appropriately sized and equipped with a reserve static line, automatic activation device, and a ram-air main parachute. Staff members who work with students must hold appropriate U.S. Parachute Association ratings, and riggers and pilots must hold appropriate FAA ratings.

Some drop zones function as a club. The skydiving club is a group of people pooling resources to operate an airplane. They share the jump plane and the responsibilities for keeping it flying. Such operations are often private and do not even offer instructional services.

When a center takes on student training a new range of responsibilities unfold. Specialized student parachute equipment is needed and this equipment needs to be stored in a secure, clean, dry area. Instructors need a quiet place for training and equipment to conducting training.

Since students in a training program eventually obtain a license, and because licensed skydivers will visit the drop zone, additional services become necessary. Reserve parachutes must be inspected every 120 days. There are inevitable rips and tears in parachute fabric that need attention. Parachute equipment needs to be assembled. The parachute rigger handles these services. This rigging concession should be equipped with a place to spread out parachutes (protected from the sun) and store tools.

A mid sized commercial drop zone may need a permanent structure like a hanger. The hanger can be used to store the airplane of course, but may also serve manifesting, packing, training, photography, and equipment storage needs. Almost any drop zone concession can operate from a hanger.

As a drop zone grows, skydivers growing with it will require equipment. Buying equipment can be a trying experience even for longtime skydivers. There are hundreds of different harnesses and parachutes on the market. Each is custom made with sizes, colors, and options. Jumpsuits serve specialized functions and are also custom ordered. An equipment concession handles these orders and helps provide customers with information so they can buy what they need to do what they want. This concession also handles less specialized equipment like goggles, altimeters, helmets, and gloves. Equipment sales often run in conjunction with rigging or manifesting services, but sometimes operate from a separate building or even completely independent of the drop zone.

Large operations need more space. There may be pavilions for packing or planning, multiple hangers, team rooms, staff quarters, and video production facilities. These outfits sport office complexes for manifesting, lounging, training, and administration. Aircraft mockups, training devices of various types, and an aircraft loading platform round out their landscape.

Coaching and photography services have their own space requirements. Video equipment needs power and photographers need
space to dub and label tapes. Coaches need a training area appropriate to their specialty. A demand for parachute packing services prompts creation of a pack-for-pay concession. This fran-
chise has its own space and storage requirements.

With skydivers, instructors, students, photographers, riggers, and
pilots running around there is bound to be need for a restroom. In
some cases the restroom is the second tree on the right, while at
some centers it's a multiple restroom complex with showers and a
sauna. Being on a drop zone all day can also make one hungry.
Parachute centers catering to a high volume usually provide a
food concession on site.

Selecting a drop zone can be a onerous task. What it ultimately
comes down to is the interest and motivations of the searcher.
What kinds of training and aircraft are available? Are there
restrooms? Is there food? There is a drop zone for every taste
and goal.

Opening and operating a drop zone requires the same planning,
commitment, and hard work as any other business. Many drop
zone's start, but only a minority survive beyond a few years.
Having the best equipment, staff, aircraft, and business plan will
stack the deck in a drop zone operator's favor. What follows is a
brief description of some staff needed to help a parachute center
run.

Manifestor
"You should be heading to the plane now."

The hub of any skydiving operation is manifest. Manifest is the
place where new skydivers register and experienced skydivers sign
up for a jump. The manifestor coordinates airplanes and people,
assigns airplane loads, logs who is on which airplane,

collects money, answers the telephone and provides information. Effective manifestors fight inertia and keep things moving. Effective manifestors understand skydiving, are able to think fast, have good communication skills, and are not afraid to exert a little professional aggressiveness in the interest of keeping the operation running smoothly.

Instructor

> *"Your maneuver was technically correct but inappropriately applied."*

"Instructor" is the entry level position into skydiving's bureaucracy. There are several instructional platforms from which to teach. Static line or Instructor Assisted Deployment (IAD) instructors guide their students through the mechanics of a static deployment method. Accelerated Freefall instructors accompany students in the air to teach and act as an additional safety layer.

Becoming an instructor means deciding, first, that you enjoy working with students and have a desire to pass on experience. It also means accepting the political requirements of entering a hierarchy. One indirectly agrees to devote potential personal skydiving time to the service of others. The skydiving instructor also agrees to stand as a representative of what it means to be a skydiver.

After obtaining a license appropriate for the desired rating, the instructor candidate completes a practical proficiency phase to learn how instructors instruct. Completing the proficiency card in this phase opens the door for a candidate to attend the Basic Instructors Course (BIC) followed by a discipline-specific certification course. Candidates learn what is expected of an instructor while completing formal requirements to attend the Basic Instructor's Course. They demonstrate the mechanics of teaching, knowledge of U.S. Parachute Association (USPA) and Federal Aviation Administration requirements, and safety in training.

12

While the BIC teaches training techniques common to all instructional disciplines, an Instructor Certification Course focuses on a specific discipline. The Accelerated Freefall Certification Course (AFFCC) is held at the national level. Local Safety and Training Advisors, S&TA's, may conduct static deployment certification courses. The most important roll for an instructor on the drop zone is to teach. But an instructor's roll goes beyond simply showing someone how to control a parachute. The student-teacher relationship is symbiotic. The most effective instructors take a personal interest in the student through the entire training process. Students gain from the teacher's experience, and teachers gain from watching their students face and overcome obstacles. Of course the student must genuinely be interested in learning for this to happen.

A graduate, once released into the general skydiving population, still needs an instructor's assistance. The heady freedom associated with being able to skydive "on your own" is too much for some to handle. Wayward novices sometimes need a gentle hand to guide them back on a safe path. New skydivers also need to buy equipment. There are over 300 different types of main canopies on the market. There are accuracy canopies, relative work canopies, canopy relative work canopies, fast canopies, slow canopies, old canopies and new canopies. Selecting a main and reserve parachute, container, jumpsuit, and other peripherals is difficult even for someone familiar with the various manufacturers and their products. It is downright mind boggling for the uninitiated.

Instructor in class

Making the leap from recreational skydiver to instructor means making a strong commitment to fellow skydivers. It is not a decision taken lightly. Instructors, more so than recreational skydivers, must look out for people, find them safe equipment to use, tactfully call them down for being unsafe, and teach them how to skydive. In earlier days a person lucky enough to find a good instructor relied on his experience and guidance through the 500 jump mark. Today instructors, even outstanding instructors, are simply too busy to coach more than one or two students at a time beyond formal student training. Finding a good instructor is just as important as finding a good drop zone, and is worth the research.

Things to ask an instructor:

Are you certified to teach this type of training? Are you current? How many jumps have you made teaching this method?

Instructor Examiner

An Instructor Examiner (I/E) is responsible for many of the same things as a Safety and Training Advisor. The I/E teaches students, guides novices, verifies qualifications, investigates accidents, and conducts certification courses. The difference between the two is that Safety & Training Advisors are appointed through a political process while I/Es hold ratings. As rating holders I/Es may perform their duties anywhere. S&TAs may work only on the appointed drop zone.

To become an I/E, the static line or Accelerated Freefall instructor must hold an FAA rigger's certificate, complete proficiency requirements, and pass an extensive eleven-part written exam. This exam is at the heart of the I/E testing process and covers safety requirements, high altitude doctrine, FAA regulations, history, parachute maintenance, records, first aid, USPA doctrine, and methods of instruction. An I/E may be rated in any training discipline.

Becoming an Instructor Examiner requires making a serious commitment to the sport. You will find an S&TA on every U. S. Parachute Association drop zone. You will not find an I/E on every one.

Tandem Instructor
"Show me a good arch."

Tandem is the most popular method for making an initial skydive. Tandem instructors brief students, assist with donning the equipment, and carry them on these jumps. After the jump, tandem instructors collect the student's equipment and pack the parachute. Tandem instructors are rated through the equipment manufacturer and must meet their certification requirements. After an extended stint as "experimental," tandem skydiving moved into its own and has been recognized by the Federal Aviation Administration as an approved form of parachute instruction.

Rigger
"What Ye Sew, So Shall Ye Leap"

Parachutes and parachute harnesses are durable pieces of equipment. But eventually even durable equipment needs attention. Federal Aviation Administration certified parachute riggers are assigned to perform this maintenance and inspection.

The Federal Aviation Administration administers criteria for rating riggers and classifies them as "senior" or "master" according to experience. To obtain a senior rigger certificate the candidate must pack 20 parachutes under supervision. Then, the candidate must pass a written exam administered at an FAA training office. Finally, the aspirant takes a practical and oral exam covering a range of rigging situations. These include packing and inspecting parachutes, sewing, repair, paperwork, and research. Passing the practical exam entitles the senior rigger to conduct the periodic reserve inspection, perform routine maintenance, and pack reserve parachutes.

Until recently, the only way to learn the art and science of parachute rigging was as an apprentice. One would find an accommodating rigger and spend several months to years learning the trade. In addition to learning reserve inspection and packing, the apprentice would pick up sewing, patching, manufacturing techniques, rules and paperwork necessary to function as a rigger. "Packers" are rigger apprentices who pack parachutes under a rigger's supervision.

This traditional approach is being challenged today by increased demand for rigging instruction. Now almost anyone wishing to learn rigging and obtain the FAA certificate to practice it has the option of attending a commercial rigging course. These courses are offered by master riggers and Designated Parachute Rigger Examiners (DPRE's) with the facilities and equipment to accommodate and train students.

A Master Parachute Rigger holds the Ph.D. of parachute rigging. Master riggers may alter parachute systems and supervise work done in a manufacturing facility. Becoming a master rigger requires 100 logged packs of at least two parachute types (seat, back, chest, or lap).

Parachutist Magazine (Jan. '98) reports that 8% of skydivers are riggers. Parachute riggers, senior and master, perform vital functions on the drop zone. They inspect, repair, and pack main and reserve parachutes. They supervise packers packing main parachutes. They teach parachute packing and maintenance. Riggers are often consulted for their knowledge of parachute designs, components, and systems. Following either the traditional path or learning rigging at a school will enrich and broaden anyone's appreciation of the sport.

16
Pilot

"I love the smell of jet fuel in the morning..."

Pilots have a responsibility for getting skydivers in the air and the plane safely back on the ground. A jump pilot must make sure FAA requirements are followed, that there is enough fuel in the airplane, that weight and balance requirements are observed, and that he or she is rated on the aircraft used.

When jump altitude is reached the pilot turns direction of the airplane over to the loadmaster or spotter and advises other aircraft in the area that jumpers are jumping. The loadmaster then directs the pilot over a suitable exit point and visually checks for other airplanes in the area (see section on spotting). After jumpers exit, the pilot descends, lands, and prepares to pick up another group.

A big part of skydiving

AIRPLANES

You and Your Pilot

A jump pilot will:

Conduct a thorough pre-flight inspection of the aircraft at the start of the day

Ensure that there is enough fuel for the flight

Know the current local weather and forecast

Have a seat belt for you and ask you to use it

Ensure that the aircraft is well maintained and fully operational

Use a sufficiently long runway

A skydiver may ask the pilot:

Are you licensed, rated, and current for this flight?
Have you checked the aircraft's weight and balance?
Is the aircraft in compliance with an approved maintenance program?
Does the weather allow for visual flight rules?

A skydiver may not ask a pilot:

To fly through clouds or reduced visibility
To allow a jump through or near clouds
To perform aerobatics or abrupt maneuvers
To place the importance of the jump over the safety of the flight
To carry more people than weight and balance or the number of seat belts allow
To fly the aircraft outside of its center of gravity limits

Making an airplane a jumpship

Not just any airplane may be converted for skydiving use. The Federal Aviation Administration (FAA) lists which aircraft may be flown with a cabin door removed in Aircraft Circular 105-2a. But removing the door is only a first step toward making an airplane suitable for regular skydiving.

To reduce weight, increase cabin space, and reduce the chance that a snag point on the airplane might catch a ripcord, seats and the right side yoke are removed. The whole airplane, particularly the interior, is checked for edges. Sharp edges that can tear or snag parachute equipment are covered up and smoothed over.

Even though an airplane may be flown with its door removed, flying without a door may not be comfortable. Air at jump altitude can get quiet cold even on a hot summer day. Pilots and drop zones have developed some ingenious methods to combat problems associated with open cabins. Jump doors have been fashioned to swing inward, swing up, slide up, be removed from the inside, and even attach with Velcro.

Aside from the necessities of having an open door and a snag-free interior there are some jump plane niceties: things that make the process of skydiving a little easier. Jumpers frequently climb on the outside of aircraft to position for exit. To aid these jumpers, handles or bars are added to the fuselage. Sometimes footholds are also needed. A clear door, or a door with a window is nice because it allows those making fine flight path corrections to get their bearings before opening the door. Thick padding and carpet on the floor help make the ride to jump altitude more comfortable while reducing potential snag points. An on board Global Positioning System makes navigation more accurate. Some jump planes even come equipped with a stereo system.

Modifications and amenities make a skydiver's movement in or on an airplane safer and the ride more comfortable, but an airplane's initial design goes a long way toward helping or hindering a skydive. One major consideration for a jump plane is the size of its door. A larger door permits more jumpers to exit at one time while aiding immediacy of contact just outside the door. A bigger door allows groups relying on relative positioning a closer initial proximity. Bigger doors also reduce snagability.

Another aircraft characteristic jumpers are interested in is the number of skydivers the airplane can carry and to what altitude it can climb. A small plane can carry four to six skydivers. A medium size plane carries seven to nineteen. And a large plane carries 20 to 40 jumpers. There are, of course, very large planes, but these are uncommon at commercial parachute centers.

Door size and carrying capacity of an airplane used for skydiving are important because these limit group size and type of skydiving. In general, larger, higher volume drop zones need larger airplanes while small operations can run well with a four-place Cessna.

A plane's maximum attainable and maximum working altitude is important because certain types of skydiving require certain altitudes. For example, a group of jumpers intending to fly parachutes for accuracy or performance are often content exiting between 3000' and 4000'. A group of Canopy Formation skydivers may have enough working time from 7500'. An Instructor-Assisted student can often satisfy the requirements of a training jump from 10,000'. And large groups often want as much altitude as they can get, sometimes even going to the added expense of using oxygen.

Small aircraft running on piston powered engines have an increasingly difficult time at higher altitudes because their power relies on oxygen-rich air for efficient operation. Skydiving operations are increasingly turning to turbine-powered aircraft to carry clients to higher altitudes.

Climb rate is a consideration for skydiving aircraft. The faster an airplane can get to its jump altitude the more jumps jumpers can jump. Many variables play into this speed-to-altitude equation, but one of the most prominent factors is engine power.

A plane's vibration and noise affect comfort. Jumpers riding to altitude sometimes need to talk. A smooth flying, quiet airplane design makes that job easier. A good jumpship design is also stable at lower airspeeds. Stability provides a solid platform for smooth exits.

As skydiving evolves, those who use jump planes grow more selective in the kind of plane they use. Increasingly modern skydivers, drop zone operators, and jump pilots are demanding more from their jumpships. They want more efficiency, stability, and safety. They also want big doors, large cabins, and a comfortable, fast, quiet ride to the altitude of their choice.

Skydiving Aircraft

Not any airplane is suitable as a skydiving "jumpship." And while some may be usable, they may not be practical. A few airplanes are novelties; jumpable, but not efficient or cost effective on a regular basis. But some aircraft designs stand out as excellent skydiving aircraft. Such an aircraft must be listed by the FAA as being able to fly with the door removed. The plane should be economical. And it should also be modified for skydiving operations.

Ideally, the door is made to open in flight (not a standard factory feature), the seats are removed or modified for space and weight, and any unnecessary protrusions like hooks, screws, or the right yoke are removed. Also, the door should be big enough to allow parachute equipped skydivers to climb out easily without snagging equipment. The aircraft should also be powerful and durable enough to climb harder and land more frequently than non-skydiving aircraft.

A few planes offer themselves as prime examples of skydiving workhorses. All more than meet the above criteria. Some have proven themselves through carrying capacity, door size, speed to altitude, or cost efficiency. Others bear the torch of durability or simply staying power.

The listing of planes that follow is far from exhaustive. There are many other excellent platforms for skydiving. But I believe these well represent the range.

Skydiving aircraft have had to evolve to keep pace with changes within the sport and the demands of skydivers. One plane has acted as a constant through this change. The undisputed backbone of skydiving and the workhorse of many skydiving operations is the Cessna 182. C-182s are durable, cost effective, and practical for most drop zones. It is a stable airplane and allows for skydiver presentation directly into the relative wind for clean, easy exits.

Most C-182's modified for jumping have the right door hinged at the top rather than on the side. This configuration allows airflow to hold the door open in flight. All the seats, except for the pilot's, are removed and padding is laid on the floor where jumpers sit. The right yoke is removed to allow more room in the cabin. Aside from its small size, a disadvantage to the 182 is its slow climb rate; sometimes taking as long as thirty minutes to carry a full load of four jumpers to 10,000 feet.

Another popular Cessna is the 206. The C-206 is larger and more powerful than the 182, carrying six jumpers and sporting a three bladed prop. The C-206 also has a right side door and can climb somewhat faster than the C-182.

A Pillatus Porter was practically made for skydiving. It has a single engine, long nose, three or four bladed prop, can carry eight jumpers, was designed for short grass fields, and has a large, cargo style door. The wing strut allows full presentation to the skydiving wind and  it is stable at low air speeds. Porters may be piston powered or turbocharged. Turbo charging dramatically improves this jumpship's climb rate.

The Beechcraft Model 18 was, in its time, a much sought-after low-wing twin-engine jump plane. It is stable, even with a large number of skydivers outside. While slow climbing, it is capable of carrying twelve jumpers to 12,500' allowing for larger formations than are possible from Porters or Cessnas.

The loud, inefficient, difficult to maintain, radial engines made the aircraft impractical for smaller drop zones. In the 1970s and '80s they were found primarily on larger volume centers or flying from center to center on a *boogie circuit*. Beech-18s have become a rarer sight on American drop zones, giving way to age and the modern skydiver's appetite for cleaner, quieter, faster-climbing rides to altitude.

Another airplane enjoying much skydiving acclaim is the venerable Douglas DC-3. The twin engined DC-3 carries fourty jumpers to 12,500' in about thirty five minutes and was considered the mother of all jumpships.

Some DC-3 owners went so far as to equip their airplanes with sound systems to help jumpers pass the long ride. Its mainliability is its small door. There are lots of skydivers inside wanting to get out and they must move single file out the door. Still, the DC-3 was used for record attempts. Even this venerable and versatile aircraft is being replaced by smaller, but more powerful and cleaner turbines.

The Beechcraft Queen Aire is still a popular piston powered twin engine jump plane. It normally carries twelve jumpers, and is found on many medium sized parachute centers. The Queen Air remains popular, despite trends toward turbine aircraft because of its efficiency and cost effectiveness.

Turbine powered aircraft are enjoying an explosion of popularity in skydiving. They are cleaner, quieter, more efficient, and climb faster than their piston driven counterparts. A turbo-prop driven airplane is essentially a jet with propellers.

The Beechcraft King Aire crosses the gap between piston and turbine powered jump planes. The main physical feature distinguishing the King Aire from the Queen Aire, apart from its engines, is merely the shape of the windows. A Queen Aire's cabin windows are square while the King Aire's cabin windows are oval. King Aires and other turbines may be supermodified to climb at incredible rates.

To put this in perspective, C-182s can take 25 minutes to reach 10,000 feet. A Beech-18 or DC-3 may require 30 minutes to climb to 12,500 feet. Queen Aires and some turbine aircraft often take 20 minutes to reach 12,500 feet. But "super" turbines can climb to 12,500' or 13,000' in ten to twelve minutes! On a busy drop zone this means more jumps in the day.

A Twin Otter carries twenty jumpers, climbs to 12,500 feet in around twenty five minutes, and has a large, left side, cargo door allowing more skydivers easier access to the skydiving wind than from a King Aire's small door. Twin Otters are rapidly becoming the turbine airplane of choice for mid to large size drop zones. More centers running Twin Otters are opting for the "Super" Otter capable of very fast climb rates.

The turbine-powered, thirty place Casa and forty place "Super" Casa offer a tailgate exit which aids in keeping a large number of skydivers close together during the exit.

Drop zones offer a wide range of aircraft, which themselves offer a range of features. Different skydivers with different needs require different things from the planes they jump. Details differ, but regardless of whether you want to build a big formation, fly alone standing on your head, or pass your Level III training jump, you need and deserve to have well maintained aircraft with experienced pilots.

Things to know and do before boarding a jumpship:

1) Know exactly what you will do on the skydive you are about to make and review aircraft emergency procedures. Know where and how you will sit, where the seat belts are located, and how you will exit. While riding to altitude mentally review the jump from A to Z.

2) Check your gear both before boarding and just prior to jumping. Ensure the leg and chest straps are correctly routed. Check that the altimeter is set to zero, goggles are clean, and the helmet fits well.

3) Stay away from propellers! Approach fixed wing aircraft from the tail and helicopters from the front. Sounds simple, but don't forget.

4) Sit where the pilot or instructor tell you to sit. Weight and balance is crucial for a successful flight. Wear your seat belt and helmet until you are high enough for an emergency exit. Avoid movement on board the aircraft which could interfere with weight and balance or snag equipment. Move only when the pilot or instructor give permission.

5) Familiarize yourself with the aircraft's door, handles, and step. Skydiving safety is a process of stacking the deck in our favor. Trying to familiarize yourself with anything in the air that you could have spent time familiarizing yourself with on the ground is not doing everything possible to ensure your best interest. The more you know and take care of on the ground the fewer things you have to think about in the air.

6) Jump run, or the final path the airplane flies before jumpers exit, is flown over an area upwind of, and adjacent to, the intended landing area. This ideal exit point is called the "spot." Spotters are responsible for selecting the spot, directing the pilot over it, and making sure the area is clear of air traffic. Instructors are initially responsible for their student's spot. Graduate and licensed skydivers are responsible for their own spot. Learn about the spotting process.

Aircraft Emergencies

Every skydive starts before you board the airplane. Before getting on the airplane you should be completely prepared for the jump ahead. This means knowing exactly what you are going to do and having all necessary equipment for preventing, or acting in, foreseeable events. Potential airplane problems fall into this category. Make sure you have helmet and goggles, remove jewelry, tie your shoes tightly and take sharp objects out of your pockets. Each jumper is responsible for personal preparedness.

Another important part of ground preparation is being ready to board the aircraft on time. Jump planes can't hold up twenty people because one isn't ready. At the start of your skydiving progression an instructor will take care of reserving slots on the airplane. It is then your responsibility to stay in the area and gear up at the appropriate time. Later it will be on your task list to know how and where to catch a ride to altitude.

Airplanes and pilots are charged with taking skydivers to a safe jump altitude. That routine goal becomes challenging when the airplane malfunctions or those involved fail to follow established procedure. These procedures lie rooted in maintenance and training and flow through the application of sound practices, awareness, and respect for aircraft.

Simply walking or standing around an airplane can get one killed if the walker is not environmentally aware. Always approach an airplane from the rear and a helicopter from the front whether propellers are spinning or not.

Moving around inside jump planes can be difficult and cramped. Guarding handles is important for preventing an accidental parachute release. Should a parachute come open in the closed cabin it should be contained. Grab it and let everyone on board know a parachute has been opened. If the pilot chute goes out an open door there is no pulling it back in. Whoever the loose parachute belongs to must exit the aircraft as quickly as possible. Everyone on board must help the person out the door. Guarding handles, avoiding making abrupt movements, and being aware of what is going on, where it is going on, while it goes on, goes far in preventing accidental parachute activations.

Center of gravity is important for stable flight. It is also important to skydivers who rely on airplanes to get them to altitude. Just as a parachute will stall when its power (drive) loses out to gravity, pilots lose control of an airplane when too much weight depresses the tail. When too much weight is too far behind an airplane's center of gravity the plane stalls, loses lift, and the pilot loses control. This loss of control may result in a flat spin, roll, or straight down drop.

Apart from premature deployments and stalls there are other problems to be aware of. The airplane can catch fire. The engine can fail. Flight control surfaces can go out of control. These are problems outside a skydiver's realm of control. Simply sitting still and listening to the most viable voice on board is the best procedure. The pilot always decides what he wants skydivers to do and may relay that decision to the loadmaster. In the event of a catastrophic in-flight failure do not panic. Panic can cause sudden weight shifts. Sudden shifts of weight can make a minor problem unmanageable.

A pilot may take one of several courses. She may decide to have all skydivers land with the airplane. This is usually done when altitude is insufficient for a safe jump. When landing with an airplane all jumpers sit down, fasten seatbelts, don helmets, and tuck their head between their knees. If there is sufficient jump altitude, and the airplane is manageable, the pilot may have some or all jumpers exit.

When making emergency exits from disabled aircraft, face 45° to the tail with both hands on a deployment handle. Exit and pull the deployment handle. Altitude and the degree of emergency determine which parachute is used. Instructors decide which parachute students use under given conditions, but the reserve is usually used when exiting a malfunctioning airplane. Reserves are designed and packed to open faster than mains and under adverse conditions.

Skydivers must not let attention and awareness wane when around airplanes. Fortunately, as with all emergencies, propeller strikes and aircraft emergencies are rare. Everyone involved with aviation must constantly work to either prevent problems, correct them, or get out of the way of those trying to correct them. Well maintained equipment with vigilant, well trained, and experienced operators, be they pilot or skydiver, gives everyone an edge on survival.

Organizer

"Get in or go in!"

The skydive organizer, a: coordinates and plans a specific goal then acts as a source of focus or motivation for others to accomplish that goal, or b: helps disparate groups find and realize a common goal. The organizer plans large formations and uses human resources to give it birth. He or she may plan challenging and interesting activities for small groups of similar experience. When present on an airplane the organizer acts as loadmaster. Sometimes the organizer collects information like number of jumps and primary discipline from those being organized then plans a skydive around the group. Sometimes the organizer plans a skydive then searches for talent to complete the plan.

Organizers have energy and charisma. They also have excellent observational and organizational skills allowing them to quickly evaluate talent and move it in a productive and rewarding direction. Gary Peek, one such organizer, explains. "Sometimes certain people fall into the organizing roll. Usually these people have a large number of jumps across a broad range of the sport and with different types of groups. They have seen skydives that have worked well, and some which have not worked well.

"Organizer types have an ability to influence others," continues Peek. "Personality plays a large roll in a load organizer's effectiveness. For some, experience is what develops the name, for others a record of success builds the reputation. And for a few, extreme tendencies or outrageous behavior act as a light attracting directionless skydivers."

Peek believes fall rate, simplicity, practice, a good exit, a relaxed pace, safety, a post dive debriefing, and fun are key elements to formulating a successful skydive plan.

Coach

> *"Perpendicular asymmetrical angularity results in vertical translational endpoints."*

A coach is a professional skydiver who teaches finer points of skydiving to anyone from graduate skydiver to world-class team. A coach is similar to an organizer in that he or she directs and motivates human resources toward a goal. But while an organizer coordinates for an event or directs several groups at once, the coach is dedicated to one person or team for one or more jumps. A team or person may use a coach to overcome a specific problem, improve overall efficiency, or learn something new. A coach is more specialized than an organizer and often has significant experience in the coached discipline.

Teams benefit from using a coach. Team coaches are often former champions passing their experience on to new teams. A successful team coach is well versed in the mechanics of the coached discipline and the psychology of performance and competition. A Formation Skydiving team, for example, might aspire to national level competition. As part of their plan to reach that goal they hire a coach who has meddled in formation skydiving at the national level. From their coach they learn tips and tricks for improving time and methods of planning for competition.

If no champion skydiver coach is available, almost anyone with an understanding of how to perform in the discipline is better than no coach. Michael Jordan's coach cannot play basketball better than Jordan, but he understands how the game is played and can offer guidance. Any team or competitive individual can benefit from an impartial and knowledgeable viewpoint.

Skydive University is a formal system certifying professional coaches. Certified coaches study goal setting, sport psychology, kinesthetics, motor skill development, skills analysis, debriefing techniques, and video analysis. Each coach candidate must make skydives "designed to practice basic air skills and learn positive video debriefing techniques."

Being a coach sometimes means staying on the ground debriefing and critiquing skydives and taking care of administrative matters. On one end of the coach spectrum is the mentor who finds reward in helping fellow skydivers find and follow a path. On the other end is the full-time champion skydiver coach with a client list. Both types of coaches and all those in between are valuable in the scheme of skydiving life.

Coaches are social leaders with the charisma and showmanship to keep people interested in what they are doing long enough to accomplish a goal larger than any single person could accomplish alone. They use a system for building a skydive which breaths life into a cold, impersonal outline. They are responsible for the motivation of a wide range of personality types and levels of experience. Mish mashes of skydiving champions, recent graduates, and uncurrent skydivers present themselves for improvement.

Skydive Photographer
"If art is to nourish the roots of our culture, society must set the artist free to follow his vision wherever it takes him." -- John F. Kennedy

Much effort and money go into the planning, execution, and review of a skydive. To get the most from this investment, skydivers rely on other skydivers to document the fleeting moments played out in the air. Action in the air is too far away to be seen from the ground and too fleeting to be remembered in great detail by participants. The skydiving photographer records skydiving images and brings them back to earth.

It was probably the lure of preserving a few seconds of excitement that prompted James Clark to take the first skydiving picture in 1927. Today's photographers have made quantum leaps since those early days of jump-click-pull. They have the advantage of hard won lessons from the past and tremendous technological advances to buoy creative spirit and technical mastery.

Photographers are key players on a drop zone. It is possible for skydivers to jump without video or photographic records, but the fleeting images recorded in the mind's eye degrade quickly and are lost to all but the most intimate participants. Photographers shadow instructors, students, and teams in whatever their discipline. Camera flyers record first jumps for later viewing with friends and relatives. Teams rely on quality air to air photography to develop more effective techniques and do them faster. Instructors use freefall images to critique students and help them learn.

Skydiving photographers play an important role on the drop zone. Accurate or aesthetic, high angle or low, side light or silhouette, in frame or out decisions are left up to him or her. There are tremendous intrinsic rewards derived from conquering composition, focus, light, and mood in the sky while falling at 120 miles per hour. The freedom of expression and a heady feeling of creativity accompany the freefall photographer as each grows into his or her own style.

By some estimates ten to twenty percent of skydivers jump with a camera to document their own or someone else's skydive. Many use the visual information they bring down to critique jumps, offer insight to others about a particular aspect of jumping, or simply for the personal satisfaction of capturing fleeting images in a challenging environment.

Photographers use a range of specialized equipment for capturing skydiving images on video and film. One distinguishing piece of equipment is the camera helmet. Skydivers need to have their hands free to maintain control in freefall and operate a parachute. Holding a camera in the hands occupies the hands, presents stability problems (both for the camera and its operator), and introduces the possibility of dropping the camera. Mounting video and still cameras on a helmet frees the photographer's hands. Specialized jumpsuits also help photographers move quickly around a subject to get the best shot. Finally, creative altitude warning devices have been developed specifically for skydivers jumping with a camera.

There are many camera helmet designs found on the American drop zone. They can be as simple as a camera taped on a helmet, to full-face, professional platforms designed to carry three or four cameras. An external video indicator light runs from the camera and is mounted just inside the field of vision to show the operator when the camera is recording. 35mm still cameras are mouth or finger activated with external shutter releases. Cameras suitable for skydiving come in ranges of quality, size, and shape. Camera flyers usually look for imaging equipment offering the best quality image in the smallest, lightest, and most easily managed package.

Skydiving while filming a skydive can be technically and creatively challenging. The camera flyer must be proficient both in skydiving and photography. Freefall photographers operate camera equipment while following the same self-preservation rules every skydiver follows. It is a difficult job. While it is beautiful and exciting to view the work of an accomplished skydiving

Camera flyer flying a camera

photographer, actually creating those images exposes one to significantly increased personal risk. Skydiving photographers can be so distracted by capturing the perfect picture that they lose survival awareness. A failure to develop balanced abilities in both disciplines puts skydiving photographers in a high risk category within a high risk activity.

The skydiving photographer's role is so wide ranging that specialties and subdisciplines have developed. Some photographers concentrate on students, some work mostly with teams, some like video, and some enjoy emulsion more. Skydiving photographers shadow teams of every make, record student training, film record attempts and competitive events, and create photographs for books like the one in your hands. Photographers have become a fixture on the drop zone and can be found on almost every airplane filled with skydivers.

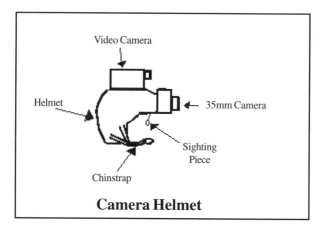

Camera Helmet

Demonstration Team

Some drop zones act as home to a team. Some teams are loose groups of friends who spend most of their jumping time with one another. Other teams dedicate themselves to touching the edge of performance in their chosen discipline. Such teams hire coaches, sport psychologists, buy matching equipment, and obtain sponsorship to acquire every possible edge.

While any team stands out on a drop zone, one team stands out on purpose – the demonstration team. Demonstration or exhibition teams dress up a skydive and turn it into a performance. Lights or smoke are used. There are streamers or flags. Sometimes parachutes are specially designed for the occasion, sponsor, or team. On the ground an announcer describes what is happening in the air, directs the audience's attention, and gives a brief bio of each skydiver. Demonstration team jumps have opened supermarkets, marked the beginning of sporting events and promoted products. The Super Bowl and Olympics both feature skydiving demonstrations.

A demonstration jump is not a normal skydive. It is a performance requiring extensive experience, planning, practice, and promotion. Members sometimes carry props and wear costumes which can interfere with equipment operation. Performers are sometimes placed under extraordinary pressure to jump despite unfavorable conditions. Also, exhibition jumps require jumpers to land in congested or populated areas, and so demand premium parachute landing accuracy skills. Only skydivers holding a PRO rating issued by the U.S. Parachute Association may jump through controlled airspace or into congested areas.

Demonstration jumps are a double edged sword for the sport. They offer great positive publicity when done well, and disaster when done poorly. A well-planned, well-executed parachute exhibition promotes events, thrills spectators, and presents skydiving to the general public. A poorly planned or executed exhibition doesn't thrill or impress anyone. Only the most current and experienced skydivers should attempt to jump away from an established drop zone.

SECTION II

TRAINING

HOW DO SKYDIVERS TRAIN?

Skydiving is trained for as a neuromuscular activity. As muscles are used to drive, walk, swim, or skydive nerve cells run a path carrying information from the brain to the muscle and back again. Muscles learn and are able to perform with improved fluidity each time the task is called upon. Developing this "muscle memory" is similar to forging a path through a jungle. Each skydiving task has its own path, and all existing paths form a web representing the totality of one's skydiving ability. As these paths are "walked" (thought about, practiced, or applied) they grow more defined and easily followed. When the paths are neglected they grow over and must be reforged.

Prospective skydiving students should select an appealing training course. Instructor rapport, desired advancement speed, cost and personal goals should carefully be weighed when deciding on an instruction method. One course might look attractive because of a lower cost per jump, but because more jumps are needed to complete it, it may not appeal to a motivated student.

Each initial training program offers advantages and disadvantages for building that web of skill paths. Once a course is selected it is important to stick with it and stay current in it. Moving from one training method to another and back again usually does more to confuse than help. Also, skydiving is a perishable skill. Three weeks without jumping makes people with thousands of jumps rusty. Going two or three months without skydiving, especially while in the fragile learning stages, produces considerable performance anxiety and increased reaction time- a potentially dangerous combination.

There are some things student skydivers can do to improve learning and reduce costly training time. First, ensure techniques are practiced true to form. Have an instructor observe practice ripcord pulls, arches, or turns. If another person is not available to watch, videotape the exercise or watch it in a mirror. Realistically simulate every movement in as much detail as possible and subject it to a rigorous and objective critique from an outside observer.

Second, learn in a safe environment. Events on a drop zone that send up warning flags should be questioned and cleared up. Third, don't learn more about injuries or anecdotes than about technique. "My friend's grandfather parachuted in the army and his parachute didn't open…" makes for an interesting story, but doesn't really relate much about the incident or have any immediate training value. Taking these stories to heart will have a detrimental effect on training because they offer tempting energy-draining distractions on which to dwell.

Related to number two and number three above, avoid learning while scared. Harboring thoughts of personal injury, or of being unable to perform at critical points, significantly reduces one's ability to absorb training. Finally, and perhaps most important, "be in the moment." We cannot effectively train to do anything when our mind is elsewhere. Thinking about an impending appointment or how much you want to get on the airplane seriously hampers training. Skydiving demands attention. Participants really are killed and injured. A failure to pay attention, not a parachute failing to open, is the leading cause of heartache in skydiving. "There are ways to get into this sport," says Charles Thomas of Sky Knights Skydiving, "99% of it is your attitude toward the learning process."

After completing initial training, and obtaining a skydiving license, a new skydiver may explore the sport within the boundaries of that license and the norms of the drop zone. While license boundaries are well defined, local limitations on new skydivers vary considerably and are points to discuss with an instructor or the manager. As we will see, it is easy to become impatient to practice new skills while lacking the experience to direct that application.

To maintain a balance between learning and stretching, and stepping out of one's personal ability envelope, requires movement with calculation and awareness. Novice skydivers, or those testing a new discipline should consult experience frequently. Books and articles have been written covering almost every aspect of the skydiving environment (see appendix). Experience also resides on every drop zone. Consulting competence in person is often better than reading about it (Oops! Maybe I shouldn't say that).

Preparing the body to skydive

Skydiving is not an overly physical activity, but planning skydives, practicing them, gearing up, skydiving, reviewing and packing four to seven times a day in the sun is taxing. There is not a great deal of physical strength needed, but being healthy and robust aids enjoyment of any sport; skydiving being no exception. In addition to general fitness there is a lot of bending in skydiving; sometimes bending and stretching in ways in which the body is not accustomed.

A flexible and healthy body significantly promotes sport enjoyment. Flexibility reduces the possibility of injury, increases range of motion, and improves fall rate control. A limber body also improves kinesthetic awareness; "feeling" the angle at the knee for example. Flexible muscles and tendons also help with packing. Active flexibility training, or tensioning, improves passive flexibility limits, or the maximum "give" a joint can take. This give reduces potential for, or severity of, injury.

There are a few rules to remember when stretching. First, it should not hurt. If stretching hurts you, you are doing it incorrectly or too strenuously. Second, hold the stretch comfortably for longer than 10 or 15 seconds. Thirty seconds is even better. Be sure to warm up slowly to the stretch. In some sports stretching is a prelude to a more vigorous workout. In skydiving stretching is the workout. Try contracting the stretched muscle without moving the limb and hold that tension for 5-8 seconds, relax, then slowly reapply tension.

Breathing properly contributes greatly to stretching activities. Muscles need oxygen and the body relaxes with controlled breathing in ways that improper breathing precludes. Breathing helps blood remove exercise by-products. The most important breathing technique to apply, whether stretching, practicing a skydive, exiting an airplane, or even driving a car under stressful conditions is to breath completely. Many of us use only a small portion of our lungs to process oxygen. Using the whole lung dramatically improves O^2 intake.

Breathing in through the nose and out through the mouth as the muscle stretches further increases stretch effectiveness. Breathe naturally and keep the abdomen soft. Control the speed and rate of each breath. The result of each exhalation should sound and feel like a sigh of relief.

When developing a personal stretch routine it is important to understand that each stretch usually works more than one muscle. Some exercises even work more than one muscle group. The order in which one carries out specific stretches can also help or hinder how well each stretch does its job. A personal aerobic and flexibility program is beyond this scope, but any of many commonly available books on the subject, will get you started.

Training principles

Controlling the physical body and the body's perceptions is important for realizing advancement in any sport. But even a perfectly coordinated mind and body can get lost without some general principles guiding the training process. How long, how intense, and how frequent one practices forms a skeleton for any training routine at any level. Skills, particularly neuromuscular skills, deteriorate quickly without frequent practice.

With that said, there is a point of diminishing returns. Training at maximum volume all the time is not a sound principle. Allow volume to increase naturally. A student skydiver might, for example, reach a learning plateau after three jumps in a day while a team bound for national competition may make ten productive jumps in a day. After a personal exhaustive limit is reached there is still marginal improvement, but the expenditure for that improvement may not reconcile with the results.

Every training session, be it for weight lifting, public speaking, or skydiving should start with a warm up and end with a cool down. For student skydivers the warm up may be physically stretching and the cool down may be a review of all skydives made during the day. For competitors the warm up and cool down may be an undemanding skydive at the start and end of the day. Training hard can be monotonous. Sometimes trying something new renews excitement. Sometimes having no specific goal relives tedium and pressure. A warm up puts one in a proper frame of mind and a cool down brings the activity full circle.

There is no cookie cutter training regimen. Each person or team reacts to training differently. Train specifically to goals while varying the routine. Don't expect shortcuts. Do whatever it takes to stay motivated, healthy, and moving the training toward realistic objectives.

The Golden Knights system for skydive rehearsal

● Walk through the dive several times. Make sure all participants know their job.

● Practice the skydive using the most realistic simulation available

● At the aircraft mock-up practice boarding the aircraft, exiting, in-air performance points, and deployment and landing strategies.

● On the plane:

√ Taxi to 2,000'   Fast repetition of performance points.
√ 2,000' to 4,000' Relax. Look outside or around the airplane.
√ 4,000' to 6,000' Mentally review the dive in real time.
√ 7,000' to 8,000' Relax again.
√ 8,000' to 10,000' Mentally review the dive with eyes open.
√ 10,000' to 12,000'   Check equipment.
√ 12,000' to Jump Run   Fast mental review.
√ Jump Run   Relax. Breath deeply.

The mind-body link

Attempting to control 100 facets of body or canopy aerodynamics at one time would be overwhelming. For any neuromuscular activity there has to be some degree of trust in the mind-body autopilot. Building a strong link between the mind and body, and learning to trust that link, is the most efficient path to learning how to skydive; but it's also the most difficult.

"Flow" is a psychosocial term used to describe this mind-body link. A good exit, for example, doesn't come from thinking about landing or even actively thinking about the exit. A quality exit comes from being in the moment of the exit while carrying all the tools needed for that moment.

Skydiving in the moment means that the skydiver is comfortable. There are no distracting thoughts stemming from doubts or performance anxieties. The skydiver in Flow has developed the mind-body link for the task or series of tasks attempted.

Being caught in Flow, whether skydiving or in some other aspect of life, is a pleasurable experience in itself and is a prime state from which to operate in a skydiving environment. But Flow is not without its limitations. One defining characteristic of Flow is a loss of awareness of anything but the task at hand--including time; a total mergence with the activity. In a less time intensive activity, like typing, cleaning, or driving, time compression or expansion may not present serious problems. In skydiving it does. Skydivers must learn to incorporate time/altitude awareness into their flow experience by scripting mind-body tasks into subroutines.

Skydiving is a movement and balance centered sport. Just like any motor activity, initial movements are likely to be stiff and mechanical. Think about learning to walk or drive a car. At first every microtask must be considered separately. "O.K., going to pass this person. Check my rear view mirror, turn on my blinker, change lanes, accelerate...," you might think. Later you do all these tasks without actively thinking because you have done them so many times that you have developed a script similar to a script for a play or a score for music.

Cross training is effective for enhancing the skydiving experience and performance. Movement centered activities like Tai Chi or Judo improve flexibility and kinesthetic awareness. Even golf improves concentration and control. Conditioning the Whole is important to realizing coordinated development in skydiving.

Skydiving requires mastery of hundreds or thousands of tasks used in combinations to create hundreds of scripts. To practice walking one needs only to stand up and put one foot in front of the other. To have skydiving exposure time one needs access to a drop zone and money to get in the air. Scripting as much as possible on the ground saves money and drop zone time.

The Package

Kinesthetic awareness allows us to stay stable belly to earth. Situational awareness keeps us from walking into a prop or opening a parachute under someone. These expressions of internal awareness must work seamlessly with elements of external awareness to produce a Total Awareness Package (TAP).

Drop zones are a microcosm of life. As such, skydivers are exposed to social, political, and cultural forces. Awareness of these forces, and preformation of appropriate responses to them, aids us in accomplishing our goals. Failing to recognize external elements affecting the skydive is failing to do everything possible to stack the deck to our advantage.

Jumping from an airplane is skydiving; just about everything else is social. How we interact with a pilot or other members of our skydiving group reflects our character, nature, and disposition. For example, a debrief is a time to review and reflect on the skydive. Dominating the review, or submitting to another's domination, reduces the debrief's effectiveness. Understanding the skydive requires cultivation of effective interpersonal skills. Understanding the difference between constructive dialog and social domination is as necessary as understanding exit transition and heading.

Politics evolve when one social group exerts pressure or influence on another. When the national parachute rigger association expands to include manufacturer and drop zone interests they have made a political move.

Certainly there is nothing wrong with political moves. They are allowable, and from the actor's point of view, prudent. But they are also political, and it is important for skydivers to view them in that light. It is also important that skydivers think about the industrial and administrative forces affecting a skydive. Refusing to accept that there are forces outside our body that shape the how, when, and where, of our sport puts control of those elements in another's hands.

An awareness of cultural forces rounds out the TAP. Skydivers arrive at the drop zone from a wide range of social backgrounds. This diversity helps create, define, and refine skydiving culture. Walter Wingwalker lent the impression of skydivers as daredevils in the 1920s. GI Joe added discipline and *machismo* to the culture in the 1950s. Sunbeam and Moonglow tempered that discipline with a spirit of rebellion and experimentation in the '60s and '70s.

Today, skydiving culture rewards those individuals and organizations which move the sport toward consumer recreation. It is certainly a rich culture; skydiving. All the cultural forces which have gone before have helped shape how we act, what we say, and how we dress on the drop zone. A TAPed skydiver will do well remembering where we came from.

Skydivers do not skydive in a bottle. Myriad forces push, pull, bend, and poke a person into a *type* of skydiver. The TAP demands the development of balance in freefall and an ability to read weather patterns. TAPed skydivers understand how politics, publicity, social interaction, dress, or speech affects the skydive and their attitude toward the skydive. In short, an aware skydiver is able to look at the big picture when necessary and separate it into pieces when appropriate.

Methods of Initial Training

Skydiver training begins with the first jump and ends with the last one. Between beginning and end skydivers climb an endless series of learning curves. Formal training carries a person through obtaining a license. After that first jump and before acquiring the license a skydiving student learns: how to handle a parachute under a range of conditions, correct foreseeable problems using accepted practices, build a Total Awareness Package, exit an airplane, spot, deploy a parachute, land, and pack up the parachute.

There are skydiving courses in which the student finds himself wearing a harness attached to the instructor's harness. There are courses beginning with parachute operation and moving gradually on to parachute deployment from freefall. There are courses which start with a general overview of the entire skydive life cycle, then build skills to flesh out that paradigm. Training methods have blended and mixed over the years. Despite this overlap, a first jump may be classified as tandem, instructor-assisted, or static deployment.

Cost is often a primary concern of people shopping for a training method. Generally, you get what you pay for. What may seem like a bargain, may actually be your worst nightmare. Training centers have significantly disparate prices and it is important to shop for the best overall package. Sometimes price differences are due to healthy competition, but sometimes a center cuts corners to reduce its price. When evaluating drop zone prices the best question may not be, "Why does this place charge so much?" but rather, "How can this place charge so little?" It makes sense that a drop zone using unqualified instructors, worn out or out dated equipment, and practicing poor maintenance is going to be able to charge less.

Progression through initial training takes many forms. There is the static line or Instructor Assisted Deployment method. There is Tandem Progression. There are Accelerated / Instructor-

Assisted Freefall methods, and any number of variations and combinations on the tandem-AFF-static deployment models. The point of any skydiving course, regardless of format, is to instill and evaluate basic kinesthetic, temporal, and perceptual skills while passing on skydiving's history and culture. Before any initial training jump (non-tandem) a student must complete a course covering the following material:

The Basic Jump Course

Drop Zone Orientation
Organizational Requirements
Equipment overview and operation
        Main parachute
        Reserve parachute
        Harness/container system
Relative wind and actions on exit
Aircraft emergencies
Equipment emergencies
        Identify malfunctioning parachute
        Emergency procedures and appropriate actions
Priorities for every jump   (ie. Altitude is never sacrificed for
                        stability)
Landing (general considerations)
        Normal landings -- Downwind, crosswind, final
        The flare and Landing Fall
Hazardous landings – Power lines, Water, Trees, Objects

Static Deployment Progression

A static line is a cord anchored at one end to the aircraft and at the other to the parachute. As the jumper exits the plane the weight of his or her falling body opens the parachute container and the static line guides parachute deployment. The static line provides very positive openings and has been used in the military since World War II. Students in a static line progression course typically make a number of static line jumps before progressing to freefalls without the static line.

Another form that static deployment might take is Instructor Assisted Deployment (IAD). Not to be confused with Instructor Assisted Freefall, IAD uses an instructor– initiated manual deployment. The key difference between IAD and static line progression is that the IAD instructor, not a static line, controls the deployment.

Sample Static Deployment Program

Phase I   - Body control and equipment checks
Phase II - PRCPs, Spotting
Phase III - Clear and Pull
Phase IV - Stable freefall, equipment lesson, and landing + lesson
Phase V - Controlled maneuvers, Packing
Phase VI - Spotting +, alternative exits, turns, loops
Phase VII- Basic relative skydiving and tracking

Freefall Progression

Accelerated Freefall (AFF) or Instructor Assisted Freefall (IAF) have similar objectives to static deployment programs: i.e. the production of a safe, and independent skydiver. But instructor assisted methods approach these goals differently. AFF/IAF offers something not formerly available to an aspiring skydiver: immediate feedback. In a static deployment program students make a jump, review and critique the jump, then make another jump to correct, consolidate and reinforce skills. Feedback is reactive. Freefall Progression students learn a little about a lot of skydiving, then later fill out their skill tool box. Students learn freefall stabilization, exits, controlled motion in freefall, spotting, canopy control, aircraft and emergency procedures, landings, and packing through a series of progressively involving levels under direct instructor supervision.

50

Custom coaching and assistance is available through all phases of the AFF/IAF jump. Using a nationally standardized training system, specialized instructors guide students through a series of progressive levels. There are seven progressive levels (not necessarily seven jumps) in the AFF program, with each building on the last. The comprehensive ground school described above precedes the first jump. Successive jumps refresh prior training and introduce new material. What follows is an outline of the basic course and a summary of the seven levels.

Sample AFF/IAF Program:

I   Introduction to skydiving
II   Introduction to rotations and slides
III Active heading maintenance
IV Active rotation and slide
V   Spotting and improved maneuver control
VI Active exit, stability recovery, tracking
VII Alternative exit, series of maneuvers

Critical Tasks at each level:

Level I

√ Exiting the airplane under control
√ Locating and pulling the main parachute deployment handle
√ Demonstrating awareness of heading and altitude

Level II
√ All level I objectives plus:
√ Demonstration of kinesthetic awareness and "trim control"
√ Assisted heading maintenance

Level III
√ All level II objectives plus:
√ Active, unassisted hover control
√ Unassisted pull

Level IV

√ All level III objectives plus:
√ Unassisted rotations and slides
√ Improved pitch, roll, and yaw control
√ Improved canopy control
√ Introduction to parachute packing
√ Introduction to spotting procedures

Level V

√ All survival objectives plus:
√ Improved hover, rotation, and slide control
√ Improved canopy control

Level VI

√ All survival objectives plus:
√ Introduction to pilot briefing
√ Active spotting
√ No-Contact exit with heading control
√ Stability recovery and tracking exercises
√ Parachute landing within 25 meters of the target center

Level VII

√ All survival objectives plus:
√ Inspect, don, and adjust equipment correctly
√ Pack own main parachute
√ Brief pilot without assistance
√ Spot without assistance
√ Demonstrate an alternate exit
√ Perform a series of maneuvers
√ Land parachute within 25 meters of the target center

Accelerated Freefall = Accelerated Learning

> ## Additional Skills needed before obtaining a skydiving license:
>
> √ Ability to perform poised and diving exits.
> √ Ability to start and stop controlled turns and individual maneuvers in freefall.
> √ Ability to gain horizontal separation in freefall.
> √ Ability to remain stable and deploy a parachute at subterminal speeds.
> √ Demonstrated safety awareness both on the ground and in the air.
> √ Ability to land within 20 meters of the target.

Tandem

The tandem serves, primarily, as an introduction to the sport, but is increasingly being used as a platform for insertion into Static Deployment and Freefall Progression programs. Tandem passengers are physically attached to an instructor through the  entire skydive (aircraft exit, freefall, canopy descent and landing).

Tandem instructors may introduce skills like altitude and heading awareness, rotations, tracking, and canopy control. Students can learn elementary skills before attempting more advanced skills in an AFF/IAF or static deployment program.

The purpose of a skydiving training program, regardless of the form it takes, is to teach students skills requisite for not being a danger to oneself or others. Each training center, instructor, and the U.S. Parachute Association, hold beliefs of how to best impart those skills. Thanks to innovation, skydivers now have a large bag of options from which to build a custom training program.

SECTION III

THE LIFE CYCLE OF A SKYDIVE

Mechanics of Building a Skydive

A large part of drop zone social interaction revolves around the planning of skydives. The plan for a skydive begins with an idea; the completed skydive being thought of as a product. It may be a simple, routine skydive idea that has been jumped thousands of times, or it may be a first-time-ever idea. Participants get together, discuss the idea, and hash out details. They then practice the plan and physically carry it out. After the jump everyone involved gathers to discuss what actually happened, and how what happened compares with the original vision. Let's look at how a skydive evolves.

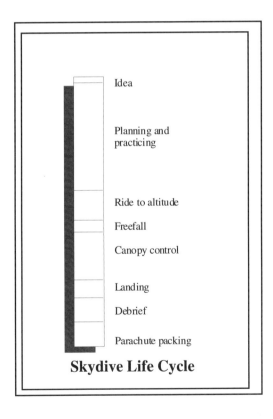

Idea

Planning and practicing

Ride to altitude

Freefall

Canopy control

Landing

Debrief

Parachute packing

Skydive Life Cycle

The Idea

The first step in preparing to skydive is to visualize what's going to happen. This conceptualization may take the form of dreaming up a unique camera exit or angle, to designing a 100 person formation, to constructing transitions between formations. Some skydives, like student training skydives, come preconceptualized and ready to jump.

Other jumps can require months in the idea-building stage. Organizers working with many people on multiple skill levels consider the "talent," or capabilities of participants. Challenges are chosen in the concept building stage which stretch each participant's ability without overwhelming it. Conceptualization requires thinking through each formation or maneuver and following it to the next until the idea is fully formed and ready for the hard planning stage.

Planning

Pre-dive planning is a time for the concept to take on a more concrete form. Planners work through the skydive verbally or on paper. This stage takes the jump from exit positions through who grips what, where, and when to how high to deploy a parachute.

Like the opening moves in Chess often determine the victor, the exit on a skydive often determines its level of success. It certainly sets the stage for the rest of the skydive. The chain of activity on the skydive determines the exit lineup which in turn exposes potential in-air traffic problems. Will person A grip person B's arm or leg? Will the Accelerated Freefall student poise or dive from the door? Will Mary have to cross Jim's path to get to her place in the formation?

Shaping the communication plan at this stage is also important. Who signals the exit so that everyone leaves together? What will that signal be? How will the instructor and student communicate in freefall? Who is in the best location for keying multiple transitions? All communications, from nods, shakes, and hand signals to eye contact must be worked out so that everyone understands what each signal means and valuable in-air learning/ performance time is increased.

A transition is movement from one maneuver to the next and takes the greatest percentage of time out of a skydive. An AFF student may transition from a circle of awareness to a 90 degree turn. Freefall Formation skydivers may transition from a Murphy formation to a Meeker formation. Canopy Formation skydivers may rotate the top canopy to the bottom position. Transitions become ripe targets for trimming. The best transitions get the right people or maneuver to the right place in the skydive in the least time.

Effective pre-dive planning smooths out the skydive, puts it in a readable form, and reduces unexpected glitches while improving confidence that the original vision is physically possible. With a physical plan firmly in hand the talent is now ready to practice, practice, practice.

Dirt Dive

A dirt dive is skydive rehearsal from airplane loading to parachute landing. This step locks the mechanical plan into muscle memory. Sequences are practiced until the skydive seamlessly flows from one function to the next.

Loading and exit, formations, maneuvers and transitions, deployment procedures, landing pattern, and special considerations like emergency procedures, grip sequence, or visual orientations are covered and rehearsed. After the plan gets locked in, each participant rehearses mentally several times before stepping to the door.

Dirt diving on creepers

Planning and practicing each skydive is essential to making the most of expensive air time. Practice also helps remove the mind from having to concentrate on mechanical aspects of a skydive and frees it to refine higher levels of performance like speed, accuracy of form, consistency, and safety. Skydiving is expensive, but dirt dives are free.

Actions at and in the Aircraft

Before boarding an airplane, every skydiver must be completely prepared to jump. This means having the plan internalized, having all necessary equipment, knowing where to sit, how to operate the seatbelt, how and when to get a final equipment check, and how to move from the seat to the door. It also means knowing what happens first, second, third and so on outside the door and where the bottom of the skydive lies.

Before boarding an airplane you should take care of the routine. Make sure that the altimeter is set to zero, goggles are clean, jewelry is removed, shoes are tightly tied, and sharp objects are removed from the pockets. All questions should be answered at this stage, and you should be relaxed but focused. Even so, if something is found missing or incorrect you can still let someone know and ride down with the airplane. Checking to be sure all tools are in the box is a part of every skydive.

Another important part of skydive preparation is being ready to go when it is time to go. Airplanes and drop zones are expensive to operate and can't hold up twenty people for one laggard. If boarding an airplane with its engines running is called for, keep a good grip on the goggles. Approach the door from the rear of the plane and stay well away from propellers – even if they are not moving.

Once on board sit as rehearsed and wear the seat belt and helmet until high enough for an emergency exit. Minimize movement in the aircraft and always protect deployment handles. Snag avoidance is an awareness packet to be cultivated and added to the toolbox starting with a first jump.

Wait for the cue called for in the plan before moving toward the door. Moving too early or too fast can upset the plane's center of gravity. Moving too late or too slow can upset the skydivers behind you. With the moment to move at hand, the airplane at exit altitude, and the door open, the people on board stop being airplane passengers and become skydivers.

The skydiving attitude

The following suggestions may assist you in a greater enjoyment of skydiving, both on the ground and in the air.

1. Skydiving is evolving at an astounding rate. As long as you are involved with it you will be learning. Come to the drop zone prepared to learn.
2. Be prepared to wait. Learning patience is part of learning to skydive.
3. Listen to your instructors. Not everyone on the drop zone is a coach or instructor. Identify the staff.
4. Everyone learns at different rates. Do not get discouraged if you do not learn at the same rate as others. Conversely do not become arrogant if you grasp some concepts faster than others.
5. Ask your jumpmasters questions. They want to help you learn, but you must let them know what you need.

Deciding when to exit

Modern parachutes are far removed from the decelerators paratroops used on D-Day, but they are still unpowered craft and are limited in their horizontal range. A skydiver cannot jump out of an airplane just anywhere over the earth and expect to land in the desired landing area. To land in the landing area requires theoretical and technical understanding of many variables.

"From what altitude will the jump be made?" and "Which direction is the wind blowing over the landing area?" are two important initial questions needing answers before an appropriate exit "spot" over the ground can be calculated. A parachute covers more lateral distance when moving in the wind's direction than it does moving against the wind. It makes sense then that the most advantageous place to exit the aircraft is upwind of the intended landing area. The faster the wind blows the farther upwind that ideal exit spot lies.

Exiting an airplane downwind of the intended landing area means opening the parachute downwind of the landing area and reducing the number of potential landing options. This may result in landing "out" and increase the possibility of confronting landing hazards (see landing hazards). Wind can blow in any direction across the landing area. It can also blow in different directions at different altitudes [*It can also blow at different speeds in different directions at different altitudes. For purposes of this discussion we will assume the wind is moving in one direction at a constant speed].

Our third question for determining the ideal spot over which to make our exit is, "What is the wind speed?" We know the exit point should be upwind, but how far upwind? Wind speed determines how far upwind of the landing area an ideal exit and opening point lies. A fast wind calls for exiting farther from the landing area than a slower wind.

These questions: how high, how fast, and in which direction, are answered on the ground during the pre-jump planning process and applied in the air as the airplane approaches the best exit point. The "how high" question is answered by asking the pilot, an instructor, or an organizer on the lift. An anemometer or a call to flight service answers speed and direction questions. Absent an anemometer, the angle of the windsock gives a good but rough idea of wind speed and direction. A straighter windsock indicates a stronger wind.

The next task is to look at an overhead photo or realistic drawing of the landing area and determine a physical reference point on the ground over which the ideal exit point rests. Fix this point and surrounding ground references in mind because they will be necessary to quickly determine the direction of airplane flight and the best fitting exit "spot" based on current wind information after reaching jump altitude.

After settling which group exits first, which exits second, and so on, the ride to altitude may be used for quiet time or as an opportunity to review the plan. Nearing exit altitude signals jumpers to start making preparations for exit. At this point goggles and helmets are donned, final equipment checks made, and the person locating the "spot", the spotter, moves to a position by the door.

Airplanes vary widely in their configurations. A wise spotter takes time to get acquainted with a specific airplane. He or she should physically operate the door. It is embarrassing to spend time trying to figure out how to open the door with a plane load of skydivers waiting to get out. The spotter also needs to communicate with the pilot. In some airplanes spotters talk directly to the pilot. In other planes, hand signals, an intercom, or a light system is used.

When the spotter opens the door he immediately looks straight down and reconciles the picture of the drop zone in his head with the observed direction of flight. An ability to look straight down is critical to the spotting process and is an acquired skill. Looking at a point on the ground that is forward, aft, port, or starboard of the airplane can result in an unsuitable spot.

The spotter should not face an alien landscape when he looks out the door. Something resembling the overhead photo studied earlier should present itself and lead the spotter's eye to the planned exit point. At this stage the spotter has two important jobs. The first is to look for aircraft below and warn the pilot if one is spotted. The second job is to locate that point directly below the plane, determine where that point is relative to the desired exit point, then watch the track the jump plane makes over the ground while advising the pilot of needed corrections to the flight path. Through this process the spotter is asking himself: Where am I? Where is the spot? Am I headed toward the spot? If I'm not headed toward the spot, how can I tell the pilot to adjust course?

As the plane nears the exit point the first group takes up positions in the door. Logistically, if more than one or two groups are exiting on one pass then not everyone will leave the plane over that ideal, predetermined exit point. In reality the first group or groups will exit on the near edge of a window of opportunity; one which still allows a landing in the primary landing area. Jumpers in the middle groups are given the widest margin of error for landing. And with good spotting practices, jumpers exiting on the far edge of the window should still be able to land in the landing area.

To maximize the efficient placement of jumper exit windows pilots are increasingly looking to the Global Positioning System for guidance. The G.P.S. triangulates satellite signals to determine a point on the ground over which the airplane is flying. Even with the aid of satellite navigation it is still crucial that a skydiver look out of the aircraft, check for other airplanes, and visually confirm the intended exit point. It is, after all, the skydiver, not the pilot, who must fly an unpowered parachute back to the landing area.

Spotting is important because landing away from the intended landing area offers improved opportunity for mishap. A rudimentary knowledge of wind, parachute, and airplane behavior lays a foundation for initial spotting efforts. A later understanding of group exit intervals develops with practical spotting practice.

Exiting the aircraft

For some, the moment of exit is the most precious part of a skydive. In many ways it's like a birth and represents an event horizon beyond which lies pleasurable tension release. An exit begins when skydivers take a "floating" or "diving" position at the door. Floaters perch outside the airplane and poise for an exit. They use bars and platforms fixed to the fuselage to help them hold on.

A floater closest to the front of the plane is a front floater, aft of the front floater is a center floater and the position aft of center float is, of course, rear float. Small airplanes, like the Cessna 182, are often equipped with a step over the wheel and a strut to hold on to. Floaters jumping this type aircraft are described as inside (closest to the door), center, and outside. Floating gives exiting skydivers the most control over their exact exit point and helps them to more easily present themselves to the relative wind.

Floater

Diver

When there are too many people in a group to fit all of them outside the airplane some must leave from inside the door. While floaters leave the plane facing the direction of flight, divers leave the airplane facing away from the direction of flight.

After positioning as a floater or diver, "timing" and "presentation" become the next bridges to cross for a successful exit. Timing is a verbal and physical means of coordinating an exit. Usually the most visible jumper in the exit lineup gives an exit count with a crisp, loud, "ready, set, go" accompanied by body movement, but almost any agreed-upon method can work. A good exit count is an essential element to a successful launch from the plane. The count should be visual, tactile, audible and at an even cadence. Ill-timed exits consume valuable freefall time and put skydivers in a mental position of trying to make up for time lost recovering from a botched exit. A clean exit sets the stage for comfortable, sequential goal completion.

"Ready, set, GO!"

The actual departure from the airplane can make or break almost any skydive. Learning to fall stable just outside the door without pitching, rolling, or yawing is one of the more challenging tasks on skydiving's learning curve. Falling stable is not physically demanding, but neither is it natural. The most fundamental freefall-stable body position is based on the pelvis-forward arch. The arch is a neutral (i.e. no sliding, turning, or rolling) freefall configuration which uses the body's center of gravity to turn

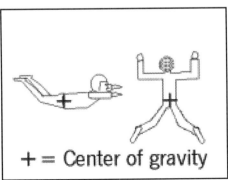

+ = Center of gravity

the skydiver belly toward the relative wind.

When the belly faces the relative wind, parachutes have the best opportunity to deploy cleanly from behind the jumper and avoid getting entangled with the body. An unstable body rolling and spinning in freefall radically increases the possibility of a parachute not deploying as designed. In the arched body position the pelvis is the most forward point. Knees are back, the head is up, the back is arched, arms are at 90° angles, and lower legs are pressed into the air flow. Holding this position deflects wind power and turns the skydiver belly toward the wind like a badminton shuttlecock's design turns its center of gravity low on its relative wind.

All objects fall with their heaviest part, their center of gravity, leading toward the Earth's center. When the badminton birdie is hit it turns around so that the rubber ball leads the feathers. A person's body in freefall is no different. Despite rumors that a skydiver's head is the densest part of his body, the pelvis is, in reality, proportionately denser. For a body to be stable in freefall (in an orientation promoting parachute deployment), the pelvis must lead. If the pelvis is forward of the rest of the body, and air is deflected evenly to all quarters, then the body naturally turns belly toward the dominating wind and does not pitch, roll, or spin.

To visualize the effects of relative wind immediately outside the aircraft, think of a tennis ball released from a car going 100 miles per hour. Following its release, the ball continues moving forward until the forward throw of the car wears off and gravity takes over, pulling the ball toward the ground. The ball falls in an arc. From the driver's perspective it may appear as though the ball is "blown back," but from the tennis ball's perspective it continues moving forward with the car's throw while simultaneously succumbing to the effects of gravity. A body in a good arch turns toward the direction of flight until forward throw gives way to gravity. Looking at the ground, swimming, kicking, and tucking up into a defensive fetal position are common novice errors at this stage and don't contribute to exit stability.

Skydivers work with, and in, wind. For skydivers, sky is the canvas, wind is the paint, and angle of attack is the brush. In freefall, the skydive's lowest common denominator is air passing around the body. When hanging under a parachute, air passing around a parachute is the lowest common denominator. How effectively a skydiver deflects that air (potential energy) is how well a skydiver skydives. All that is relevant in skydiving is the relationship between the body, or parachute, and the air.

Many games depend on winning openings for successful conclusions. Skydiving depends on smooth, coordinated launches and stable bodies to lead goals toward realization. Novice skydivers often grapple with the kinesthetic coordination of different body parts. Later, they fumble with the complexities of relative skydiving involving multiple bodies. The two appear different, but both rely on common principles. For stable group exits, everyone in the group must be stable as they slip into the relative wind. Good timing allows everyone to leave together. Skydive Arizona's Safety and Training Advisor, Bryan Burke, advises, "Think of the air as a friendly environment, slip into it smoothly as you climb out of the airplane. Arch, take a deep breath, open your hands, and float off on the wind!"

Outside the Door

We've examined planning for a successful skydive and the body's relation to the relative wind. Now let us look at space and time; because, in skydiving, space equals time and time equals space. Prior to the exit skydivers are falling at zero miles per hour. As soon as a body leaves the airplane it starts eating up altitude. Just outside the door a skydiver falls through the first thousand feet in about ten seconds, then balances with air density and burns up altitude at a constant rate of about six seconds per thousand feet. These numbers are approximate and minor variations in individual terminal velocities may be accounted for before leaving the ground (see later discussion of space and time and fall rates).

Putting aside the common idea that all objects fall at identical rates, in the real world two elements affect bodies in freefall or under canopy. They are drag and gravity. Gravity is a given. As long as we are within the Earth's gravitational field we are going to fall toward its center at 32 feet per second per second. This means that in the first second we fall 32 feet, but in the second second we cover 64 feet and so on.

Without the atmosphere, falling objects would fall faster and faster until they reach the surface of the earth. With the atmosphere, that speed is capped by a terminal velocity, or maximum fall speed, which can be altered by a diver's clothing, position, or canopy.

With an atmosphere, skydiving suddenly becomes infinitely more enjoyable. Our atmosphere contains tiny particles which drag against objects being pulled through it by gravity's force. The longer these particles stay in contact with a body, or the more particles that are in contact at any given time, the more the body slows. When the atmosphere comes into play, as it must in any skydiving equation, a body in freefall will initially accelerate then reach a balance between the friction of the particles in the air and the pull of gravity.

We can't control gravity, but there are things we can do to control how long those particles stay in contact with our body. By doing so we can change or refine our terminal velocities so that groups of skydivers can fall at the same rate and stay level with one another. When multiple skydivers are on level they are said to have "levelitity."

Terminal velocity is constant, but initial airspeed is a different story. As a person steps out of an airplane, he or she is already moving at airplane speed, so accelerates only about 20 or 25 miles per hour. This existing motion coupled with minimum acceleration reduces the roller coaster effect commonly associated with dropping from a height. Also, because of the relatively high altitudes involved, ground-based perceptions skew and leave little feel of falling. Falling freely through the air from a normal skydiving altitude is more like floating on a firm cushion than hurtling toward the Earth.

A skydiver's heading in freefall forms from an imaginary line drawn from the body's center to a reference point in the field of vision. A ground reference is found on the horizon, an aircraft reference is found on the airplane (immediately after exit), and a skydiver reference is found on another skydiver in freefall. These references are baselines used for heading changes, loops, rolls, or hover control.

The center of a skydive, called the center point, is that point in space averaged from all bodies in freefall. A solo skydiver holds the center point in the belly, just below the navel. Two skydivers have a center point equidistant between them. Add a third body and the center point gets pulled off to one side or the other.

Flying the Body

A body's motion while falling free through all those little particles may be symmetrical or asymmetrical. A symmetrical body deflects air equally to all quarters. The center point doesn't slide forward, backward, or to the side in space and the body holds a heading.

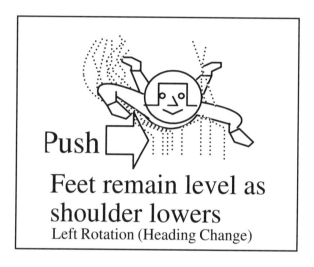

Push

Feet remain level as shoulder lowers

Left Rotation (Heading Change)

Asymmetry results in a rotation (heading change), roll, loop, or slide. The asymmetrical body deflects more air in one direction resulting in an equal and opposite movement. The skydiver intentionally applying asymmetry may direct airflow to slide sideways, forward or backward, rotate along three axis, and move up or down relative to another body in freefall.

The neutral, stable flight position described in the prior section turns the body belly toward the relative wind, but there are many ways to fall through the air and still deflect air symmetrically. Skydivers have been playing with symmetrical and asymmetrical presentations for a long time and have refined them to a remarkable degree. Student skydivers first master symmetrical presentation then progress through heading changes (turns) and translations (controlling fall speed). To turn, the body pilot may, for example, lower a shoulder slightly in the desired direction while keeping the lower body flat. This twists the upper body into a sort of propeller shape, deflecting air asymmetrically across the chest. The body changes heading in the direction of the lower shoulder.

Any number of contortions produce the same effect. Lowering a shoulder is just one example. To stop a turn on a new heading the body returns to neutral after possibly counteracting momentum with a quick turn in the opposite direction. If lowering a left shoulder rotates the body counterclockwise then what would extending the legs do? Right! A slide in the direction of the head. Extending legs increases drag on the lower body, tilts the skydiver slightly head low, and deflects air toward the feet pushing the body in the opposite direction.

Translating up or down relative to another skydiver calls for either cupping air to slow the fall rate or exaggerating the pelvis forward body position to increase fall rate. Controlling fall rate is a necessary part of relative freefall skydiving because real skydivers (as opposed to ideal or textbook skydivers) have varied fall rates constantly in flux. While necessary, fall rate compensations in freefall should be kept to a minimum.

Spotting. Altitude. Heading. Fall rate. Presentation. Stability. Sliding. Timing. Whew! Overwhelming. Yes. There is a lot to think about. The good news is that not all of it is presented on a first jump, and some things which are presented do not require absolute mastery for many jumps to come. Of course some skills, like altitude awareness, should be fired in the kiln of understanding even before the first jump. Other skills harden as exposure time increases.

Fall Rate

Group skydiving requires the skydiver to control fall rate. A skydiver properly compensating for fall rate is level with other skydivers in the group. Eliminating too-fast or too-slow fall rate differences while staying in the middle of the fall rate range is the first task for any group wanting to fall relative.

A fall rate is expressed as a range between the fastest and slowest one can fall and still maintain control. Fall rate differences occur when one skydiver presents more or less weight, or more or less surface area, to the relative wind than the rest of the group. For example, with all other variables held constant, a short, heavy jumper falls faster than a tall lightweight. Ideally, a given group of skydivers will fall comfortably in the middle of their collective fall rate range while remaining level.

To get closer to this ideal, lightweight skydivers can don tighter or smoother jumpsuits to speed up when jumping with heavier friends. Heavier skydivers can slow down their fall rate with larger or more porous jumpsuits. Some people, because of body composition and flexibility, have a wide range and can fall very fast or very slow. Some have a narrow range. You can see by the illustration at left that person «C» in a neutral body position would not be able to skydive effectively with person «B» without some help from a jumpsuit. Person «A», with a little assistance either way, could skydive with either «B» or «C».

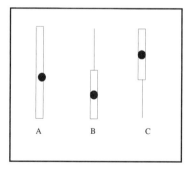

Piecemeal groups unfamiliar with one another's fall rate can size up fellow group members and dress to compensate for fall rate differences. A group may also take a few minutes to share personal measures of relative speed. By dividing total weight, including gear, by height squared (weight/height^2) each person gets a number describing his or her fall rate. This number becomes meaningful only when compared with another jumper's number. Ignoring the decimal and first zero, and assuming other variables are held constant, the person with the larger number will fall faster than the person with the lower number. Armed with this information each member can put on an appropriate jumpsuit or otherwise prepare fall rate expectations.

w/h²	66"	67"	68"	69"	70"
150#	0.034435	0.033415	0.032439	0.031505	0.030612
155#	0.035583	0.034528	0.033520	0.032556	0.031632
160#	0.036730	0.035642	0.034602	0.033606	0.032653
165#	0.037878	0.036756	0.035683	0.034656	0.033673

Sample graph of fall rate indicators

Despite prior preparation, fall rate differences happen. Should a jumper start to sink relative to the group, he or she could slow down by slightly raising the pelvis, lowering the thighs and chin, and cupping the shoulders. Going low on a group and not knowing where other jumpers are is a seriously dangerous aspect of formation skydiving and is an area to cover thoroughly with an instructor. Floating, or gaining altitude on a group, is the other side of the coin. To correct this problem exaggerate the pelvis-forward attitude— tighten the gluteus maximus, stick the chest out and keep the head back.

Learning to fall in the middle of the fall rate range while adjusting that range to compensate for a group is requisite to effective freefall formation skydiving. By taking measures to control weight and drag before boarding the airplane, level flight maintenance becomes less difficult. And once fall rate problems are removed, the freefall portion of the skydive becomes less complicated and more satisfying.

A freefall formation skydive where all participants fall in the middle of their individual fall rate range while remaining in the middle of the collective fall rate range is an ideal and utopian condition. The reality is that skydivers constantly compensate for fall rate differences with body position. How much compensation a person requires is testament to his or her preparation and skill.

After the Freefall-- the Bottom End

Parachute deployment altitudes are set during the planning stages. From the moment of exit until reaching that planned deployment altitude, skydivers must maintain altitude awareness. Once the planned altitude is reached we have reached an important, some would argue the single most important, point on any skydive – parachute deployment.

Opening altitudes are assigned to allow skydivers time to ensure that they land under an open parachute. Conventional reasoning is that as skydivers accumulate experience they develop improved awareness and decrease reaction time in an emergency. Jumpers intimately familiar with equipment and emergency procedures may safely work in freefall a little lower than jumpers not so familiar.

Loss of time and altitude awareness while coddling distractions is a major contributor to skydiving fatalities. No distraction is worth dying for. Every time you do anything in freefall, intentionally or not, check altitude. That way a distraction such as a difficult maneuver, hand signal from an instructor, or loose goggles won't induce altitude awareness problems. In freefall there are no time outs. The clock doesn't stop for thought. That's why planning, preparation, and muscle memory are so important. S&TA Burke drives the point home. "The main thing to remember about altitude is that if you run out while in freefall you die." Skydivers must be aware and prepared to deploy a parachute at any point on a skydive- from the moment of exit to the preplanned opening altitude.

Statistics indicate that the most dangerous part of a skydive comes from landing a fully functioning parachute. Yet there are a surprising number of skydiving fatalities testifying that a failure to deploy either parachute in time also results in injury and death. Why would someone be unable or unwilling to deploy a parachute? Knowing what altitude one is at and performing appropriately at key altitudes is called altitude awareness, and its cultivation forms a part of the core of skydiver training.

Planned activities on the freefall portion of a skydive generally are carried out at higher altitudes shortly after leaving the airplane. As a skydiver loses altitude and approaches the planned deployment point, margin for error and focus of attention correspondingly constrict.

Looking at the illustration below you can see that at higher altitudes a skydiver might check the altimeter, complete two or three objectives maneuvers or goals, then check altitude again. In the middle of working altitude the aware skydiver might check altitude after every objective or given period of time. As the skydiver approaches the close of working altitude, she must be continually altitude aware. All tools are used to this end. Of course the altimeter is a primary tool. Knowing how to read the altimeter helps too. There are also a range of electronic audible and visual altitude awareness devices as well as a few internal awareness devices.

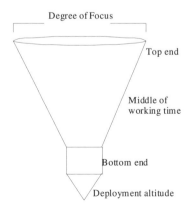

One internal system developed over time is peripheral awareness: the computation of one's angle relative to the horizon. This angle starts out relatively sharp and flattens during descent. With practice a skydiver may calculate this angle using peripheral vision and only minimal awareness. Another internally cultivated method for gauging altitude is temporal awareness. Temporal awareness is an estimation of time in freefall. This internal clock sends an alarm saying, "Wake up and check your altimeter," or "Pull!" A lack of experience or currency, or jumping from different altitudes can distort both temporal and peripheral awareness.

Altitude awareness is critical and the loss of it is life threatening. This problem compounds when a skydiver is running out of altitude, is unfamiliar with equipment, and has trouble deploying a parachute. Add to this the possibility of a malfunction at the resulting low altitude and you have a recipe for disaster.

Parachute Deployment

With an understanding of when to deploy, skydivers need to know how to initiate deployment. The deployment process is straight-forward: track for separation, visually clear the air above and below, signal intent to deploy, free the pilot chute, confirm pilot chute deployment, and return to neutral freefall. Let us look at each phase of this process.

Tracking for separation

Clearing air begins by gaining separation from other skydivers as called for in the plan. Some skydives call for close proximity deployments. As long as a close-proximity deployment is planned for it can be carried off safely. Unacceptable risk quickly blossoms when one unaware skydiver wanders over another unaware skydiver in freefall. This blossoming may unfortunately bear fruit when both of these jumpers reach their planned deployment altitude. A horizontal (flat) track for separation physically clears the air. Learning to track flat and on heading is a survival skill.

After separation, skydivers signal an intent to deploy while simultaneously looking over the shoulder and back as far as is possible without losing stability. The universal signal of intent to deploy is a double wave--crossing and uncrossing the forearms twice.

The next movement in the deployment sequence is a reach for the main parachute deployment handle. As one arm reaches back for the handle, the opposite arm simultaneously pivots at the shoulder so that the hand is in a line extending forward from the spine. Once located, the handle is extracted according to the demands of the equipment and objectives of training.

A check for pilot chute deployment is similar to clearing the air over the back: turn the head to look over the shoulder. This accomplishes two things. First it acts as a check to visually see

The Reach

that the pilot chute is inflated and guiding deployment. This movement also improves the pilot chute's ability to inflate and guide deployment.

Lastly the jumper returns to a neutral freefall position and awaits canopy inflation. If time lapses without a telltale tug on the shoulders and noticeable deceleration (usually a count to four or five) then emergency procedures should immediately be initiated (see "parachute malfunctions" section). Once the parachute is exposed, air enters through its nose and is rammed into the closed back end. Deceleration begins in earnest and the skydiver becomes a parachutist. A check is promptly made directly overhead to determine the parachute's condition.

The sport parachute system, called a "rig" in skydiving jargon, includes two canopies and a harness/container assembly. Deployment starts when a pilot chute enters the relative wind. The pilot chute acts as an anchor in the air while the jumper continues to fall. As pilot chute and jumper separate, the container opens and a small bag containing the parachute lifts into the airstream. The parachute's suspension lines are drawn off this bag until fully extended. The bag then opens and the canopy spills out and begins to inflate as the cells fill with air. As the canopy inflates, a small rectangular piece of fabric, called a slider, slows inflation speed as it slides from the top of the suspension lines to their bottom. Ram-air parachutes open much faster than round parachutes because of their significantly smaller size. Too-fast parachute openings have been the bane of the design and can damage both jumper and equipment.

The list of possible parachute malfunctions is long and will be covered in greater detail later. At this stage understand that a functioning ram air parachute has three characteristics. It is square (four sides and four corners), it must be stable (flying straight), and it must be steerable (under control). Remember what to check for by remembering these three "S's."

Open Canopy

The first two Ss are determined at a glance, "Is it square and stable?" If a parachute is functioning properly it will open and fly straight ahead at twenty to thirty miles per hour. The last check, steerability, is determined, first, by releasing brakes stowed on the back of the risers and, second, by turning the parachute. Pull both steering handles, called toggles, down to full arm extension then return them to their original full-up, full-flight mode. Brakes are set at about 50% on ram air parachutes to slow down deployment speed and prevent the canopy from surging forward during the opening. They *must* be released before steering can be checked. This movement may also be used to check flare control.

To check steering to the left, pull on the left steering toggle. The canopy should start to bank into a left diving turn. The degree to which the toggle is pulled determines the speed of this turn. A toggle pulled to chest height, for example, turns the canopy at 50% speed. It is important to understand that a turn's full speed is not instantaneous. It takes time to accelerate to a given toggle command. To stop the turn, return the toggle to its full-up position. Repeat this process for the right turn. While turning, it is a good idea to look at the ground and orient to the landing area.

Line twists, end cell closure, and stuck sliders are nuisances easily corrected from under the main canopy. Hanging under a canopy with line twists is similar to sitting in a swing, and instead of swinging, spinning around. Line twists barber poll the suspension lines and have several causes. It is important to clear line twists before checking steering. After recognizing that the lines are twisted but the canopy is square and stable, pull outward on the risers and pump the legs like riding a bicycle. This speeds the untwisting process.

End cell closure occurs because air has not inflated one or both canopy end sections. A cell closed canopy is still stable and steerable, but the leading edge to the uninflated side flutters or rolls under. To inflate the cells manually, pull down on both toggles, hold them for a second or two, then return them to their full up position. This pumping maneuver forces air through and inflates the affected cells.

Sometimes a slider will begin to descend spreading suspension lines and get stuck half way down. At the half way point there is less outward line tension forcing the slider to its full-down position. As with end cell closure, full canopy control with a stuck slider is still possible as long as all "S" checks pass. An offensive slider may be pumped down just like the end cells are pumped open.

After clearing line twists, a stuck slider, or end cell closure, continue resolving questions of location: "Where am I relative to my intended landing area? Which direction is the wind blowing across the landing area?" and, "Am I upwind, crosswind, or downwind of my intended landing area?"

Having clear air for parachute deployment eliminates a sizable percentage of potential problems associated with this critical point. Tracking, waving off, reaching, checking, and gaining canopy control are skills developed early in any training program. After opening, gain canopy control, clear line twists, lower the slider, inflate the end cells and check for canopy function.

EMERGENCY PROCEDURES

In a Nutshell

Emergency procedures lie at the core of skydiver training. Instruction for handling foreseeable equipment emergencies is covered in any respectable basic jump course. Less "routine" emergencies are deferred for a later time either because of time constraints or because there are no commonly agreed upon procedures for handling them. Basic survival skills for equipment, aircraft and landings are the first ones covered. These are reinforced throughout formal training.

It is currently a widely accepted practice to teach the three "S's" as a means for determining if a ram air parachute is functioning and landable. Is the parachute symmetrical? Does it have four sides and four corners? Is it flying on a heading in one direction, or is it whipping about and spinning without regard to skydiver input? Does it turn to the right and left on command? Does the skydiver have control of it? If the parachute passes the three S checks - "square," "stable," and "steerable" - it is probably a functioning and landable parachute. If it does not pass the three S checks then the jumper may be under a malfunctioning main and should follow emergency procedures appropriate to his or her experience, training, and equipment.

The Long Version

Skydivers sometimes classify equipment malfunctions into categories. High speed, low speed, total, partial are terms used to describe the condition of a malfunctioning main parachute. Still, the fact remains that a malfunction is a malfunction is a malfunction. Malfunctions of the main parachute require swift and appropriate procedures for safely deploying a reserve. These procedures vary widely by equipment configuration and situation, but all hold some traits in common.

The most effective emergency procedures are simple and reliable. Any number of plans for handling the maze of equipment problems may prove effective, but actively thinking through scenarios and physically practicing emergency procedures before facing an emergency is the best way to develop a set of personally meaningful responses.

A properly open ram air parachute is first square. It is not really square, but skydivers call ram air canopies square because "square" is easier to say than "rectangle" and the term distinguishes ram airs from round parachutes. The square parachute should have four sides and four corners. It should be symmetrical: the same on one side as on the other.

The canopy should be stable. That is the canopy should fly straight ahead and not independently turn from the heading it faces or otherwise act in an uncontrollable manner. Finally, the canopy should be steerable. The canopy pilot should have control of the parachute.

If a parachute is not square, stable, or steerable then it may be malfunctioning and emergency procedures resulting in a reserve activation may be justified. No one wants to leave a landable main parachute for a reserve. Doing so reduces the probability of landing safely. However, there should be no hesitation if emergency procedures are needed. Lost time results in lost altitude which results in a narrower margin for error.

The fastest credible malfunction a skydiver may experience is the *total* malfunction. Total malfunctions come in three forms. One type of total occurs when the skydiver has reached the parachute activation altitude and attempted to pull but cannot locate the main deployment handle. A second type of total occurs when the handle is located, but the jumper has difficulty pulling it. The final way a main parachute can completely fail is when the jumper locates and pulls the main handle, but the container remains locked. Basically, if a jumper has reached the assigned opening altitude, attempted to pull, and is still in freefall, he or she is experiencing a total malfunction.

Once a parachute pack, called a container, opens and pulls the bag holding the parachute into the airstream, the skydiver's descent begins slowing. When this "deployment bag" rises from the container the parachute's suspension lines unstow. If these lines were to unstow, and for whatever reason, the parachute remained locked inside the deployment bag, the jumper would be descending with a *baglock* malfunction. Should the bag, pilot chute, bridle, lines, or any section of the system catch a body part, like an arm or leg, it would hook the parachute and create a *horseshoe* malfunction. Horseshoe malfunctions are considered by many to be one of the most difficult to successfully clear.

When the suspension lines extend to their full length, and the deployment bag opens, it spills the canopy into the airstream. Should the exposed canopy refuse to catch any air the jumper is said to be trailing a *streamer*. Streamering parachutes are far from landable. They are certainly not square. They are not stable. And there is no steering or control.

Another malfunction, somewhat slower in nature, occurs when the parachute comes out of the deployment bag and begins to inflate, but doesn't inflate completely. The inflated part begins driving forward while the uninflated part drags. This causes the canopy to spin in the direction of the dragging side. A *spinning* parachute does not make flat turns. It dives as it turns, increasing the rate of descent, decreasing control, and providing an unacceptable landing speed. For the *total, baglock, horseshoe, streamer*, or *spinning* malfunctions a correct, timely, and fluid emergency procedure is the only corrective action.

A possible emergency procedure decision point occurs when both main and reserve parachutes have deployed at the same time. If *two canopies* have inflated and one parachute is directly behind the other and both are facing in the same direction then emergency procedures are usually not needed. Both parachutes may be landed by steering the frontmost parachute. If, however, both canopies are inflated and begin to separate, interfere with each other, or one begins to spin then equipment and training-appropriate emergency procedures are called for.

Line twists, end cell closure, and stuck sliders are more nuisance than malfunction and the remedies for them have already been covered. Line twists are relatively common. Hanging under a canopy with line twists is similar to sitting in a swing and spinning around. The line twisted parachute is still square and stable with the lines barber polled up from the risers. It is important to remember that brakes should remain stowed on the back of the risers until the line twists are cleared. If control lines were released and pulled down, the twisted lines would lock them in their down position and possibly cause the formerly square and stable canopy to stall or spin.

End cell closure occurs because air has not inflated one or both canopy end cells. A cell closured canopy is still stable and steerable. As long as the parachute passes its steerability check it may be safely landed. This same rule applies for a stuck slider.

The main parachute activation handle (Ripcord or pud) may be located in any of a number of places on the harness. It may be on the legstrap, on the hip, on the belly, or on the bottom of the container. Emergency handles are on the main lift webs in the front. These handles should be visually locatable and easily reached, but far enough out of the way so as to not snag accidentally.

Most licensed skydivers choose a two-point emergency system, with one handle serving to release the main parachute and another activating the reserve. There are as many solid reasons for using two-point systems as there are for using single handle systems, but two-point systems currently dominate the market.

The Cutaway

While far from standardized, equipment configurations have tended to conform to the market's buying patterns. For this discussion of equipment operation I will use the most common configuration; the duel handle system. This system has one handle affixed to the front of the harness which, when pulled, releases the main parachute. On the opposite side of the front of the harness rests the reserve activation handle.

The *cutaway*, or *breakaway*, is but one tool in a box of emergency procedures. But it is a big one. The cutaway is used when there is tension on the risers, but no serviceable parachute. Streamers, baglocks, and spinning malfunctions easily fall into this group. Malfunctioning main parachutes are released prior to reserve activation because they could easily interfere with the reserve parachute's deployment.

To cut away, visually locate the main parachute release handle. Peel the handle off its Velcro and pull it down and away, ensuring that the cables are clear. You might want to visually locate and grip the reserve handle before activating the release, but don't remove or pull it until the main canopy has jettisoned.

Next, if you have not done so already, locate the metal reserve deployment handle on the opposite side of the harness. Hook the thumb into the handle and pull it to the full length of the arm. It is important to keep both eyes on the handle being pulled so as not to lose it. Practice at locating handles under a variety of conditions is part of any training or currency program, but in an actual cutaway one cannot afford to miss a handle in a panicked grope. Eyes on target. Move the body in the direction the eyes are looking. Release the main. Open the reserve container.

While the two-point system is the system of choice for many skydivers there is another option for reserve parachute activation. The Single-point Operation System, or SOS, is the system some instructors choose for their students and the choice of some licensed skydivers. SOS equipped harnesses use one handle for both the main canopy release and reserve activation functions. One handle simplifies the two step operation of "cut away-pull reserve." A single handle also eliminates the possibility of pulling the handles in the wrong order. One reason many skydivers desire two-point systems is because they jump with faster flying parachutes and are subject to faster acting malfunctions. It may be better, under some conditions, with a radically acting and uncontrollable parachute, to release the main and regain some stability before deploying the reserve. This is not an option when using an SOS. Camera flying and canopy formation skydiving offer two examples of disciplines which may require a release well before reserve activation.

For most malfunctions requiring reserve activation the procedures are to release the main parachute then immediately deploy a reserve. Dispute arises when discussing procedures for a total malfunction. Experience has shown that following the cut away-deploy reserve sequence has been most effective for meeting the simplicity requirement of an effective procedure. With one procedure a jumper does not find himself falling at 120 miles per hour at 2000' thinking, "Hmm, should I cut away first or just deploy the reserve?" The argument against cutting away for a total malfunction is that pulling a cut away handle requires more time than simply pulling the reserve activation handle.

Equipment emergencies may be experienced whenever one deploys or attempts to deploy a parachute. They occur for a variety of reasons, in a range of speeds, and each demands its own most effective procedure performed in sufficient time/altitude. Loss of altitude awareness is easy when focusing on and fumbling with a malfunction rather than applying a learned procedure. Thinking about and trying to tame a malfunctioning main parachute while losing altitude is dangerous and an unnecessary cause of injury or death. It is every skydiver's responsibility to understand the range of possibilities and what to do with them.

Canopy Control and Performance

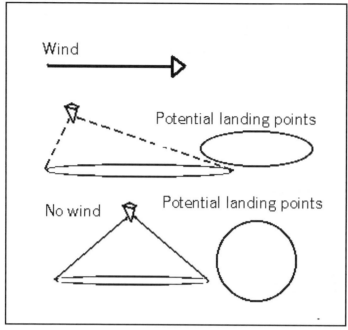

Wind Cone

Constant practice, combined with a grasp of theory, leads to consistent canopy control and landings. The lines holding the parachutist to the parachute also hold the inflated parachute in a slightly nose-low attitude. This angle, called an "angle of attack," deflects air toward the parachute's tail and drives the canopy forward. In effect the parachute slides forward through the air at around twenty-five miles per hour while descending at some eight miles per hour. Skydivers sometimes refer to this forward speed/descent rate as a ratio. This example parachute would move forward three point one feet for every foot of descent giving it a 3.1:1 glide ratio. As long as both control toggles are at their full-up position the parachute's airspeed remains constant.

Canopy control is both the immediate, selective canopy manipulations and the entire flight pattern. In short, everything influencing the mechanics of turning, slowing, speeding up, or landing is canopy control. So is the process of constantly sampling the environment and planning contingencies. To exercise immediate canopy control to change heading a parachutist pulls down on the toggle to the side of the desired turn. The amount of toggle pull dictates the speed of the turn and corresponding degree of dive. Ram air parachutes do not make flat turns. Rather they dive into the direction of the turn. To stop the turn on the new heading the parachutist returns the lower toggle back to its full-up position.

To slow a parachute's forward speed, both toggles may be depressed. A problem with significantly slowing down is a loss of control. The ram air parachute is a wing and needs lots of air flowing over its surfaces to maintain lift. When a canopy is slowed, it loses lift until a stall results, at which point it begins descending more than moving forward. A *flare* for landing is a controlled stall with judicious expenditure of forward speed in exchange for extra, short-term lift. The landing parachutist smoothly and evenly pulls both toggles to their full-down position at a height off the ground that results in a complete loss of lift (stall) just inches above the ground.

Landings

Let's start this important section by examining a textbook, theoretically perfect, landing. A parachute landing area may be divided into a series of imaginary lines and points that help with navigation. Some lines remain fixed while others move relative to the fixed references.

For this model to work, for the landing to be perfect, we must assume quite a few variables as given. We must first assume that the parachutist is operating in that ideal funnel shaped window, called the "playground," located upwind of the intended landing area. A playground is what the spot becomes once a skydiver opens a parachute.

Second, we are assuming that the wind is not shifting and that it is blowing at a constant rate over the landing area. Wind blowing over the landing area forms an imaginary line passing through its center. If our wind shifted, this line would pivot on a point at the geometric middle of the landing area and make a compensation to the landing forecast necessary. We will call this geometric center the "target."

Now our parachutist is under a fully open and properly functioning parachute, in the middle of an ideal playground area. Looking down, the parachutist recognizes physical reference points from the overhead photograph and mentally establishes the playground's boundaries.

Now is the time to complete any pre-planned canopy exercises assigned by an instructor or to explore the range of a canopy's performance on one's own. While so doing it is important to maintain a vigilant awareness of altitude. Things may be happening slower now, but the parachutist must be aware that turning or other maneuvering increases altitude loss which can quickly accumulate and catch one off guard. Flying a canopy can also be a lot of fun and offer a rich source of distraction – distraction which can draw one away from the primary job of landing in the landing area.

Drop zones often take measures giving student skydivers a maximum amount of space in which to learn canopy control without having to deal with the problems associated with a canopy collision. One key to avoiding canopy entanglements, and a good habit to get into, is to look in the direction of the turn and continue looking in that direction until the turn is complete.

Some level of awareness should also be devoted to staying in the playground. Parachutists who do not land in the intended area frequently land off because they were not paying attention and flew (not "drifted") out of their maneuver window. Then upon realizing their error they find they are too low to correct it.

Three awareness points for the playground are now in play. One needs altitude awareness, awareness of other parachutists, and a feel for the limits of the playground. Our third assumption then, and this is a big one, is that the parachutist is aware of all three – vertical position, horizontal limits, and proximity to other objects in the air.

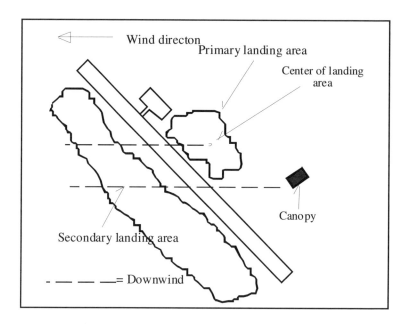

Activities in the playground make up the first phase of landing the parachute. Once the parachutist reaches an altitude from which he may successfully enter the second phase, the landing pattern, he leaves the playground area behind and flies downwind toward the target. Flying in the same direction the wind blows is called "running." The altitude for this departure varies with equipment, location, and wind conditions. It will be 1000' for this illustration.

At 1000' our ideal parachutist turns the canopy to face downwind and covers ground to an imaginary line running perpendicular to the windline and passing through the target. This line divides the landing area into upper and lower, or upwind and downwind halves.

After passing this line into the downwind portion of the landing area the parachutist must be especially vigilant and not penetrate too far downwind. To do so invites the possibility of not being able to penetrate back upwind. A failure to fly far enough downwind also results in not landing in the target area.

To land in the intended area the parachutist must fly far enough downwind so that when he turns back to face the wind he covers only the distance from that turn-in point to the target; no more and no less. Herein, then, lies our fourth assumption. We are assuming the parachutist knows how far his parachute will fly under a range of wind conditions.

For our purposes, the farthest downwind of the downwind/upwind dividing line the parachutist should fly is another fixed imaginary line marking the downwind edge of the clear landing area. This line is called the "baseline" and represents a downwind boundary beyond which the parachutist may not be able to return to the target. Canopy control skill is demonstrated by arriving at the baseline with altitude to spare. Excess altitude may be bled off, but altitude can never be added.

For this discussion our perfect parachutist arrives at the baseline

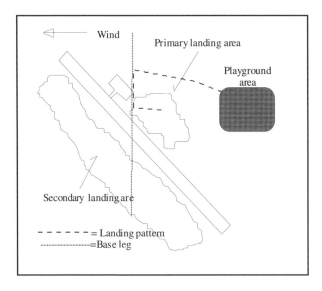

from the playground at 700'. Seeing he is approaching this barrier, he begins making the required 90° turn. Parachutes do not make instant turns. Delaying to begin the baseline turn until reaching the baseline puts the canopy pilot too far downwind. So our fifth assumption will be that the parachutist has turned on an appropriate baseline.

Now the parachutist flies along the baseline perpendicular to the windline. From this point to landing the parachutist takes altitude cues from the environment. Peripheral awareness, depth perception, angular judgment, and the perceived size of known objects begin to take precedence over altimeter use at this stage in the landing process. Altimeters are designed to read thousands of feet and grow more difficult to read and less accurate when trying to distinguish hundreds or tens of feet. In the early learning stages a ground crew assists landing skydivers, but it is never too early to begin developing height awareness skills.

The point over which the canopy pilot turns to face the target from the baseline is all-important. The final 90° turn into the wind is the culmination of all canopy control which has come before and dictates to a large degree where the parachutist ultimately touches down. This critical point is reached by bleeding off excess altitude while flying along the baseline.

After making the initial 90° turn at the baseline the jumper flies to the target's windline and makes a visual estimate of height and distance from the target. If the estimate is that, from the current height, the parachutist can cover the distance to the target (and no more), then the decision to make the final turn is well placed. If, on the other hand, the estimate is that turning to face the target would result in flying over the target then the decision to continue flying along the baseline and burning up excess altitude is the correct one. Should altitude need bleeding, then the parachutist turns 180°, "S"-turns, at the side of the landing area, and heads back along the baseline.

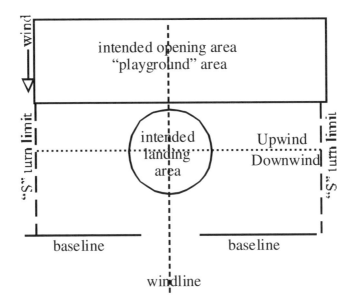

To "S"-turn, a parachute pilot continues flying along a baseline to the side limit of the landing area then turns 180° back toward the opposite landing area limit, making the turn toward the direction of the landing area (i.e. not turning his back to the wind). Once again upon reaching the target's windline the canopy pilot makes another estimate of height and distance. He either turns 90° toward the target, or continues along the baseline for another "S"-turn at the other side. The assumption then, our sixth, is that the parachutist is capable of estimating height and distance well enough to make that last 90° turn toward the target. Of course our textbook parachutist is doing well and headed for an accurate landing. He continues "S"-turning until around 300' when he makes his final turn toward the landing area.

While our perfect parachutist is doing well, not all landings proceed so smoothly. Chronic undershooting, landing short of the target, or overshooting, flying over the target, characterize early canopy control efforts. Overshooting occurs when the parachutist makes that final 90 degree turn either too high or too close to the target. Undershooting results from making the final turn too low or too far downwind of the target. Both under and over shooting may confront the parachutist with hazards to landing.

At around 200', or whatever the drop zone standard is, no more turns may be initiated. The parachutist is now committed to the landing. All the canopy control that can be done has been done. Hands and toggles are in the full-up, full-flight position, eyes are at 45° to the front, and the parachutist is preparing for the landing flare. Our seventh and final assumption is that the parachutist has developed depth perception and timing sufficient to resolve the flare point.

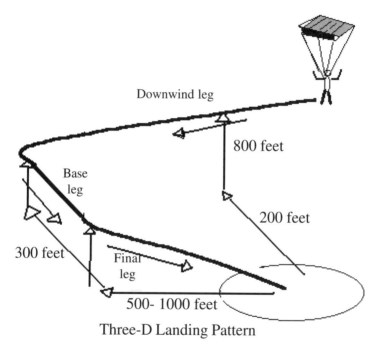

Three-D Landing Pattern

The flare is one skill only practice can develop. In the early learning stages many centers advise students on flare application. Eventually, though, skydivers must wean from this assistance and flare on their own volition.

A flare is the smooth redirection of air over the canopy's surfaces to simultaneously slow forward speed and temporarily produce extra lift. Though flare application begins and ends along a wide spectrum dependent on parachute loading, parachute design, induced speed, and altitude density, for purposes of this illustration our parachutist will flare at 12' (with his feet twelve feet off the ground).

Mechanically, the flare is the smooth and even movement of both steering toggles from their full-up, full-flight position to a full-down, full-braked position. Flaring too soon or too fast results in reaching the apex of the flare before touching the ground and subsequently losing that magical substance, lift, which keeps a wing flying. Having lost lift, the parachute can only stall and drop the parachutist to the ground. Flaring too late or not at all results in reaching the ground with excess energy moving at an angle into the ground. Flaring neither too high or too low delivers a soft, step-down landing.

Theoretically a flare is complex. Scientists have studied it. Theorists have written theories about it. But those involved in its practical application know how good it feels to have all of a parachute's energy dissipated, hang motionless two inches above the ground for just a moment, then step down effortlessly onto solid earth.

Our example of a perfect parachute landing is an ideal, but there are precautions that real skydivers may take to hedge bets in the likely event all the assumed cards don't fall into place. One is to locate alternate landing areas after gaining canopy control, and commit to one after determining location and working wind conditions. Another is to check the parachute's penetration into the wind. A faster wind dictates a baseline that is closer to the target, while slow or no wind might convince the parachutist to push the baseline a little further downwind.

While the 90° turn to approach the target should be absolute and set the canopy pilot on a course straight into the target area, there is wiggle room. A parachutist above 100 feet (or local standard) can still make minor turns of 45° to 90°, called sashays, to bleed off a little altitude and prevent an overshoot. Other canopy control tricks may be used to prevent undershooting if that's needed.

Landing away from the intended landing area is certainly not ideal, but is a normal part of skydiving. It separates skydivers into two groups: those who have landed off, and those who will land off. When landing off the main landing area one should keep priorities straight and play all safety cards. As much as possible land in a clear area facing the wind, make no turns below 100 feet, and roll upon landing while keeping the feet and knees togeather. Commit to a landing area, primary or secondary, while high enough to carry out a proper landing pattern. Landing problems can almost always be traced to a failure to select an appropriate area, commit to it, and carry out an acceptable landing pattern.

In high winds the canopy may stay inflated after the landing and begin dragging the parachutist across the ground. Pulling down on one toggle will turn the canopy toward the ground, collapse it, and keep the jumper from being dragged. As soon as possible, gather the canopy into the arms and head to the drop zone or a pickup point. Often pickup points for an off landing are at the nearest road. It is exceedingly frustrating for searchers searching for a missing jumper to find out, after a massive hunt, that he or she decided to take a cross-country hike instead of walking to a road.

To review: a successful canopy pilot quickly determines the wind's direction and speed then locates upwind and downwind segments of the landing area and his or her relative location to these elements. The landing area's wind line pivots at the center of the landing area to reflect the current wind direction and a parachutist may be described as upwind, downwind, or crosswind of the landing area's center point. Exiting an airplane and opening a parachute upwind of the intended landing area gives a skydiver an upwind advantage and increases margin for error.

To ensure an on-target landing, parachutists fly their canopies to a staging area called a playground area. There are a variety of patterns used for normal landings from the playground but the most widely accepted landing pattern is similar to one airplanes use when approaching an airport. The canopy pilot turns downwind and flies to the baseline: an imaginary line perpendicular to the wind line and downwind of the target.

A final approach is made from a height that the parachutist knows will carry him or her into the target area. If a final is turned from the baseline too high, or the baseline is too close to the landing point, the jumper will overshoot the landing area. If the turn-in to final approach is too low or the base leg is too far from the intended landing point the canopy pilot will undershoot the landing area.

If a final approach is high, "S" turns of 180° doubling back across the base leg reduces altitude and leads to a more accurate landing. "S" turns should not exceed the width of the landing area and canopy pilots should be prepared to turn on final at any point. Parachutists get one final approach. They cannot apply power, pull up and bring the canopy around for another try.

All skydivers should remain alert and watch where they are flying. Lower jumpers have right of way over higher jumpers both in freefall and under parachutes. If, for some reason, two skydivers on the same level were headed straight at one another, both turn right to avoid the collision.

At the end of the journey is the flare for landing. The concept is easy, but the application is sometimes challenging and requires practice.

Landing in a clear area

Remember, there is only one landing per canopy flight and there are a few rules to make each landing safe and soft. First, leave the toggles all the way up until ready to flare. It is a common novice error to slow canopy speed during the final approach. A slower canopy speed may feel more comfortable, but it offers less energy for flaring. A ram air canopy may be landed safely at half brakes (toggles at shoulders or chest), but this does not provide for an optimum landing (see "A Word About Canopy Speed").

Second, do not flare too high. Novice skydivers often get nervous and flare too early forcing the canopy to its stall point. Flaring too high is bad, but going back to full flight after flaring high is even worse and results in a recovering dive into the ground.

Third, do not flare too low. Flaring too low does not give the canopy an opportunity to slow down and the parachutist would land with too much angular speed. Fourth, smooth, fluid flares allow the canopy to slow down with more control than a fast flare. Fifth, never land in mid-turn. Turning dives the canopy and dramatically increases descent rate.

Flaring is a critical skydiving skill requiring timing. Actual flare points vary with wind conditions and canopy. Quickly learning and applying the rules for effective flaring reduces the number and severity of difficult or hazardous landings.

A Word About Canopy Speed

Ram air parachutes translate forward speed into additional lift when flared for landing. It stands to reason that the more speed a canopy possesses, the more potential lift is available for selective application during the flare. A canopy's inherent forward speed comes from its design and attack angle. This speed is set at the factory. There are ways, though, to alter a canopy's attack angle to artificially increase speed and lift for landing. The trade off for this added energy is, unfortunately, a narrower flare window and subsequently decreased margin for error.

Experienced skydivers sometimes practice techniques for inducing landing speed. They are impressive to watch, but are not something for someone learning the basics to imitate. Let's look at some ways to alter landing speed starting with techniques offering the widest margin and moving through to those with the narrowest. The first landing is not as much a flare as it is a mush. In a mush the canopy pilot slows the parachute and rolls out the landing.

Slowing a canopy to half brakes, putting the feet and knees together, and rolling along the side is reasonable and prudent and offers the widest margin to compensate for inexperience or unusual conditions. This half-braked landing slows the canopy without generating additional lift.

The straight-in approach with a normal flare is the next step up in the speed-for-landing continuum and offers the best balance between producing lift and having a cushy margin for error. Flaring at 10-12 feet will generate lift to reduce rate of descent while simultaneously stopping forward motion.

Any maneuver applied to a canopy that increases speed for lift beyond that designed into the parachute is *induced speed*. Induced-speed landings offer a narrower margin for error in exchange for improved lift. A two riser maneuver, during which both front risers are pulled down on the final approach, increases speed for landing while offering recovery for the flare.

Turning to land is another way to induce speed for added lift. Turning to land using a single front riser offers even more speed than a duel riser maneuver. But as the angle and severity of the turn increase, the margin for error proportionately decreases.

Toggle-turns for landing are considered by many to be unnecessary, and unreasonable. Some skydivers unfamiliar or uncomfortable with riser maneuvers initiate toggle turns in the belief that they have the same effect as riser turns. A problem with toggle turns is that they require more recovery time than riser turns. This means that an offset toggle approach must be executed higher than a riser approach to allow the canopy time to recover before reaching the flare point.

Artificial speed for landing reduces margin to either side of the flare. Flaring too early gets to the apex of the flare faster and results in a stall. Flaring too late leaves the canopy with lots of speed headed at an angle, sometimes a steep angle, into the ground. Losing a toggle or letting a riser slip out of a hand while inducing speed for landing is a recipe for disaster. Good judgement, a logical progression of experience, practicing techniques high in the playground area, and consulting experienced canopy pilots when deciding to make a canopy go faster than it was designed will carry one far.

Landing Emergencies

☞ AVOID them! Land in a clear area. Keep a long stretch of grass to your front.

☞ Feet and knees together

☞ Land in/on obstacles at half brakes (toggles at shoulders)

Trees:
    √ Put the feet and knees together
    √ Cover the face and throat with the forearms
    √ Do not try to climb down (wait for help)

Water:
    √ Put the feet and knees together
    √ Remove or loosen the chest strap
    √ Hold the breath and do not panic
    √ Do not flare over the water
    √ Get out of the harness under water and swim away
    √ If you land in moving water swim down and upstream

Power Lines:
    √ Put the feet and knees together
    √ Fly parallel with the lines
    √ If suspended off the ground wait for power to be turned
        off

Other obstacles: - buildings, airplanes, cars, etc.
    √ Put the feet and knees together
    √ Assume an L shape with legs together and out in front
    √ Slow forward speed appreciably
    √ Strike side of obstacle with feet and roll to one side

Only one thing is guaranteed in skydiving. If you jump from an airplane you will land. With proper training and equipment most parachute landings will be uneventful. But just like we do for equipment and aircraft emergencies we must think about, train for, and otherwise prepare ourselves to address the hazardous landing.

Normal landings are made facing the wind in a clear area. A hazardous landing is any landing that is not normal. Landing going cross wind or downwind is hazardous. Landing in trees, power lines, water, or on buildings is also hazardous.

Parachutists reduce a canopy's ground speed for landing by facing the wind. A crosswind landing results in sideways movement. A downwind landing results in ground speed which may be too fast to control. Even so, landing in a clear area while facing crosswind or even downwind is usually preferable to landing in or on hazards.

Trees offer one example of a potential hazardous area. Failing avoidance, turning to face the wind while covering the face and throat and putting the feet and knees tightly together is the next best option. Keeping the feet and knees together is important because one does not want tree branches coming up between the legs. And keeping the feet and knees together offers advantage should the parachutist go all the way through the trees and land on the ground. Two sticks are easier to break one at a time than when held together. Legs are easier to break when apart than when held together.

Water is another example of a potential hazardous landing. Just like a tree landing, reduce forward speed by braking the canopy 50 percent and facing the wind if possible. Put the feet and knees together and be prepared to roll on landing. The water may be shallow or there may be objects just under the water. Rolling along the side with the feet and knees together, elbows touching and chin tucked offers advantage over trying to stand up in unknown waters.

After landing safely in the water, shed the equipment and swim out from under the parachute. Do not surface into the canopy. Instead, swim down and away from the equipment. If the body of water is moving, shed the equipment and swim down, up stream, and away.

Power lines are the most hazardous of hazardous landings. Nylon, the material parachutes are made from, will conduct electricity at high enough voltages. Avoiding power lines is paramount. Should avoidance fail, then flying parallel to them is the next best option. Flying parallel to the lines reduces the possibility of getting entangled while increasing the possibility of slipping through to the ground. Having the feet and knees together, ready to roll, reduces potential for injury.

Power lines can collapse a canopy. If they have captured a part of the canopy and are suspending the jumper off the ground then the best option is to wait for qualified assistance. No one should be allowed to touch the suspended jumper until power is turned off.

Hazardous landings also include landing downwind, crosswind, or on solid objects like buildings, airplanes or cars. An alert canopy pilot uses planning and evasion to avoid hazards. But finding oneself committed to a hazardous landing is survivable. Slow the canopy to half brakes, keep the feet and knees together, roll out landing, and be ready to get clear of further harm in the safest manner possible. Practice for hazardous landings by mentally rehearsing a variety of creative scenarios and talking with skydivers who have encountered them.

After the Landing

Landing safely is a rush. When all the hundred elements of a skydive come together there is serious cause for celebration. But the post landing euphoria must be tempered with awareness. Jump for joy, but don't jump on the canopy. Throw arms wide and wail with excitement, but don't let go of the goggles or helmet. Turn eyes to the sky wide with wonder, but watch for other landing parachutists. Don't remove equipment in the landing area. Keep everything together until back in the equipment area.

Debrief

No skydive is full circle without a debrief. The debrief is a group effort. Every person involved gives a first person account of what was seen from that perspective. As in many other aspects of life it is best to give people a chance to say for themselves, "I fell short here," or, "I'm proud of this."

The post skydive critique is where skydivers learn the most. Each participant goes through each performance point noting deviations from the original plan. Critiques are held shortly after the skydive and excitement levels can run high, but each person must be allowed uninterrupted time to describe the action from his or her perspective. Only one person should talk at a time during the debrief. Two people trying to make a point cancel one another and waste daylight. A mediator is helpful for moving a critique along when it goes awry. When talking (even to yourself, in the case of a solo skydive) start with positive aspects: what was learned, what was exceptionally interesting etc.. Next discuss what could be personally improved. It is important to keep an order to the comments. It's easy to start thinking about the exit, get distracted, go straight to the landing, then natter about the ripcord pull. If necessary take a break after removing equipment to jot down the flashbulb images and put them in order.

After each person has had a say, the group reviews video of the jump if it's available. After the debrief, when the pieces of the puzzle are clearest, each person records them in a logbook. Post dive critiques allow each skydiver to know how he or she performed and help to develop that indispensable survival quality: awareness.

Critiquing Body Position With Video

John Hamilton, in his article on debriefing, expounds the benefits of video for dive recall. "Debriefing skydives with video is one of the most effective tools we have to use in learning how to perfect our air skills." Video of a solo skydive can even help improve kinesthetic awareness.

The advantages of video are obvious--perfect recall and critiquability. Many sports use videography with great success to enhance athletic performance. Tennis, field sport, football, and baseball players regularly review and critique videos to improve individual and team effectiveness. A study of wheelchair athletes analyzed body positions using freeze-frame video. Computers compared observed body positions with an ideal model and offered suggestions for adjusting it to more closely match the ideal. According to the study, those athletes who used this system significantly improved their performance over a control group.

One doesn't need a high tech computer to benefit from kinesthetic video analysis. A VCR, a piece of plastic, a grease pencil, and an all sides video can achieve the same thing. The first step is to get a centered, full-frame video showing all sides and over the back. After the jump tape a piece of plastic over the monitor and freeze the video at each position- front, side, and top. With video frozen on the screen, mark a dot on the top of the head, chin, neck, elbow, wrist, hip, knee, ankle, small of the back, and shoulders. Connect the dots, making a stick person out of the video sample.

The next step is to measure the stick figure angles and compare these observations with "ideal" angles. Shoulder, elbow, and neck angles form 90°, the crotch angle is 45°. A 175° measurement runs from between the shoulder blades, to the small of the back, to the back of the knees, and from one elbow, to the center of the chest, to the other elbow. These measurements give us the arch angle. The knee angle is 105°. List corrections, in degrees, needed to match the ideal then practice making those corrections on the ground with someone watching, then make another skydive concentrating on weak areas.

SPORT AND COMPETITION

Skydiving is a sport in the sense that there is competition between individuals and teams. There is game in skydiving, but a sport is more than just game. As Andrew Cooper, author of *Playing in the Zone*, explains, a sport involves history and memory. "When we speak of baseball as a sport we mean more than a single instance of its playing." The same holds true for skydiving. When we speak of skydiving as a sport we are really talking about the history, situations, collection of games, and people which together make sky diving skydiving.

Some skydiving competitions are an outlet for individual expression while others reward disciplined teamwork. Likewise, some meets are formal, following rigid judging criteria, while some are little more than a friendly game of tag played in the sky. Most competitive scoring is spread over several jumps, or rounds. After completing all scheduled rounds, each competitor's points, time, and penalties are added or subtracted.

The U.S. Parachute Association organizes collegiate and national competitions. States or groups of drop zones also form competitive circuits. There are planned local competitions and impromptu, spur-of-the-moment games. Each discipline is represented at every level of seriousness and organization. Investigating these avenues can be intoxicating and care should be taken to not allow desire to participate overcome training or common sense.

<u>Summary of the Game</u>

Skydiving is a participatory sport pursued actively by thousands in local, regional, national, and international arenas. Each competitor has a parachute rig, jumpsuit, goggles, an altimeter, and other periphery items as needed for the given discipline. There are currently 7 recognized disciplines in which competitors may participate. They are the classics: Style and Accuracy; modern team events: Formation Skydiving and Canopy Formation Sky-diving; and formative or experimental events: Freestyle, Freefly, Skysurf and their derivatives. While we will discuss each of these in turn, for purposes of understanding skydiving competition in general, we will use Formation Skydiving as an exemplar. Formation Skydiving competitors may form teams of any number, but usually in groups of 4, 8, 10, 16, or 20 jumpers. A game, or meet, is played out over a series of jumps, or rounds, and may last several days.

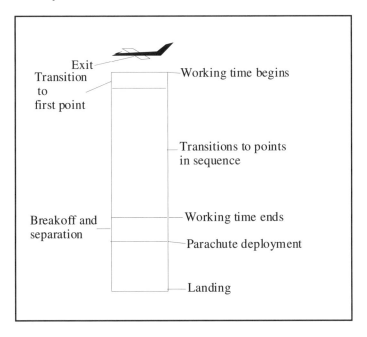

The Vertical Field

Skydiving is played on an ethereal and relative field. There are no out of bounds or goal lines, but there is a top, bottom, start, and finish. Each team operates within the confines of working time beginning at the moment of exit and ending with the expiration of an agreed upon time. Teams, consisting of players, a photographer, and possibly a coach, plan and rehearse safety and strategy prior to each round.

Team members must be familiar with every other member's position, yet hold a specialty. In Freefall Formation skydiving there is a front float, center float, rear float, and diver exit position. Any team member can fill any position, but excels at one. The same holds true for positions within a given formation or transitions between formations.

Prior to each Freefall Formation skydiving meet, the meet director draws formations from a pool. Teams score points when they successfully build the drawn formations in the order they are drawn. Each team member must be in the correct slot with the correct grips for the point to count. A "bust" results when a member breaks a grip and starts moving to the next point before all grips are taken. The penalty for a bust is, at a minimum, lose of the busted point, and the following two successful points.

Competition is ingrained into our species. It pushes us to push ourselves to excel as individuals and collectively. Skydiving is

competitive, but is more intrinsically competitive than many sports. Skydivers compete against themselves using past performance as a yardstick to measure present performance. When, in a competitive arena, they use other skydivers as a yardstick. It is not uncommon to see competitors at skydiving competitions helping opponents. Skydiving competitors want those competed against to be in their best form so as to serve as a valid measure. This spirit of sharing and camaraderie pervades skydiving and is one factor attracting many to the sport.

Forms of competition in skydiving are limited only by the imagination and skill of participants. Naturally some forms of competition have grown to be more widely accepted than others. Five forms of competition are accepted worldwide: Accuracy, Style, Formation Skydiving, Canopy Formation Skydiving, and Freestyle.

Classics- Style and Accuracy

Skydiving can trace its sport origins to the classics- Style and Accuracy. Style and Accuracy represent the genesis of skydiving for a purpose beyond exiting the airplane, falling for a while, and deploying a parachute.

Canopy Accuracy requires maneuvering a parachute to land as close as possible to a predetermined point on the ground. It demands a number of skills to do successfully. One must be able to determine wind speed and direction at varying altitudes and exit over a suitable exit point. After exiting and deploying, the accuracy jumper flies a parachute toward the landing point.

Landing accurately is an important skill in itself and should be practiced on every jump. But the degree of expectation for competitive accuracy has changed as equipment developed. When round parachutes dominated, accuracy competitions were measured in meters. Modern equipment and training allows skydivers to commonly land within centimeters of dead center (as measured by an electronic scoring pad). Differences between national level competitors frequently come down to foot placement.

Style is an individual competition emphasizing speed and form. Stylists exit the airplane and perform a "series" of turns and backloops for time. Competitors must remember which series is being performed, leave the airplane so that ground based judges can see the maneuvers (with a special scope), and execute crisp maneuvers. A time penalty is added if the stylist does not return to the original heading, over rotates on the backloop, or does not perform the correct set. Style brought a whole new element to skydiving competition- freefall.

Video Telemeter at Style Meet

Modern Team Events- Freefall and Canopy Formation Skydiving

Freefall Formation Skydiving

Not long after the popularization of Style did skydivers discover the challenges of maneuvering one body in close proximity to another in freefall. This relative freefall, later called Relative Work then Freefall Formation Skydiving, developed in the late

1950's. The challenge initially was to get as many people as possible to build a linked "formation" in freefall. Later, the challenge was to build as many different sequential formations as possible on the same skydive or during ever larger formations. Each completed formation earns the team a point, with points totaled over several jumps.

The number of points any given group may accumulate is largely dependent on the number of people in the group and the available working time. National competition is broken down into four person, eight person, ten person, and twenty person formations called "ways" (eg. 4-way, 8-way etc.). Entire formations of four, eight, and sometimes even ten are routinely taken right off the airplane. This arrangement saves valuable time which may be used for building the first formation. In fact an entire sub-discipline, Ten-way Speed, competes on the time from the exit to the first formation.

Twelve Way Freefall Formation

Canopy Formation

Canopy Formation competition takes two forms: rotation and sequential. In rotation, teams form a stack of parachutes for a first point. One point is awarded when all team members have joined the stack. The top parachutist then moves to the bottom position for an additional point. Sequential Canopy Formation teams, like freefall sequential teams, build a series of formations within their working time and are awarded a point for each one successfully completed.

The starting point for either form of canopy work is the two-stack. The upper jumper in this two parachute stack, called the base, slows canopy speed while the lower jumper, the pin, adjusts speed and approach angle. The object of this maneuvering is to contact the base's legs with the leading edge of the pin's parachute. On contact the skydiver flying the base position snatches the lower parachute's leading edge and engages the suspension lines with the feet. At this point a two-stack forms and further canopies may dock or the original two may transition to a new formation.

A side-by-side, for example, forms from the two-stack when the base-pin pair compress the stack and move to grip one another's harness. They then guide the two parachutes side by side. From this configuration, the base-pin pair may hook legs and separate their parachutes further so that both canopies and pilots face the ground. In this dramatic configuration, called a "down plane," parachutists can reach speeds of 60 miles per hour straight down.

Sequential Canopy Formation competition is formatted much like Freefall Formation Skydiving. Competitors build a series of preplanned formations and a point is awarded for each successful formation.

Canopy Formation skydiving requires additional skill sets. It demands no less planning, concentration, or communication than Formation Skydiving, Accuracy or Style. Building canopy formations also requires more physical strength than most other skydiving disciplines. Gaining a base of general skydiving experience with an emphasis on canopy control while seeking the advice of experienced Canopy Formation skydivers will lead one to many happy, safe, and fun jumps hooking canopies together.

The Skydiving Team

Skydiving teams require dedication, commitment, discipline, and planning. Team members should regularly meet to discuss their goals. Goals should be as clearly defined, challenging, and as realistic as possible. For example, "We are going to compete in some meets this year," would be too vague a goal. "We are going to compete in this year's state intermediate competition to place in the top four teams," would be a more specific goal. Every team member should understand the goal and be able to internalize it as worthy of the personal sacrifice necessary for its realization. The team goal should represent a realistic assessment of collective ability.

A team must also have a plan for accomplishing their goal. The plan should break down the goal into smaller, more manageable tasks. "We will strive to improve our personal best at each meet and treat practices as though they were mini-meets," is an example of goal breakdown. Next, team members should create a training regimen. Notes on a calendar help tremendously here. Indicate training and rain dates. These dates should logistically work for all team members. Members should discuss money available for training, agree on a number of training jumps per practice, and the focus of each practice. Coaching, wind tunnel practice, trips to other drop zones, photography, and personal issues might also be addressed in team meetings.

Successful competitive skydivers follow the FIT model, standing for Frequency, Intensity, and Time, to help plan training. Frequency refers to the number of training units. These are the number of days devoted to team practice. Intensity is the number of jumps, or degree of jump difficulty. Time is how long training continues without a break. It is possible to jump-pack, jump-pack, jump-pack without pausing to review video or eat lunch. With packers and multiple equipment sets it is even possible to jump every time the airplane takes off. At some point the team reaches training saturation beyond which more is not productive and might even be counterproductive.

Beyond these basics, team members may decide if buying matching equipment, and hiring a dedicated camera flyer or a coach looks promising. Matching equipment adds to team solidarity and enhances the psychological edge. Any team jump recorded on video is equal to three without video. Access to a champion skydiver turned coach is optimum, but any disinterested advisor with a grounding in training and theory can effectively critique team jumps and help improve performance. Additionally, coaches may handle routine administrative tasks like manifesting and co-ordination for packing or video services.

Modern Individual Events

Freestyle / Freefly / Skysurf

Aside from style or accuracy what can a solo skydiver do on a skydive? Freestyle skydiving developed, in part, to answer this question. Skydivers were looking for a way to broaden the spectrum of solo freefall possibilities. Mike Michigan, Deanna Kent, Tamara Koyn and others experimented with alternative relative wind presentations.

Skydivers learned how to remain stable on their side or back, while sitting, splitting, or doing lay-ups (full body length rotations). These freestyle pioneers learned to do splits and "daffys" in freefall. They could stand up, change heading, and stop on a dime. Over time freestyle developed rules and has become accepted as a competitive event.

While freestyle may be done alone, competitive freestyle is not really an individual event. It is done with a photographer. The camera flyer is responsible for composing the shot and framing the background, both of which tally into the overall score. The freestylist completes a series of movements in front of the camera which are judged on precision, originality, creativity and aesthetic appeal.

Skysurfing is also competitive. The skysurfer must stand on a surfboard in freefall and complete a set of compulsory exercises demonstrating control, including forward and backward rotations, rolls, and turns. Then the skysurfer performs a signature series of maneuvers and combinations.

Freefly differs from freestyle in its rejection of formal competition and acceptance of relative flight. Freeflyers build relative formations while standing, sitting, or even on their head in freefall.

Skysurfer

In sum, skydiving competition is comprised of the classics – Style and Accuracy, modern team events – Freefall Formation Skydiving and Canopy Formation Skydiving, and modern individual events – Freestyle and Skysurfing. "Freeflight" catches just about anything else one can do after leaving the airplane and before deploying a parachute.

Competitive Mindset

Skydiving competition is no different from other forms of competition. There are winners and losers; scores, points, judging, and high drama. The skydiver begins competing from the moment he or she steps on a drop zone. This competition with the self is the strongest form found in the skydiving game. There are a few ingredients in the constructive competitive character worthy of review in a book about skydiving.

First, regardless of pursuit- business, school, work, family, retirement, sports- one must have a goal. A definable objective or purpose is the light at the end of the tunnel without which one wanders aimlessly in the dark. Purpose is most effective when accompanied by a thorough understanding of the limitations imposed (rules) and the degree of effort involved. For example, jumping from an airplane offers obvious time limitations. "What must I do within these time limits to be competitive?" one might ask.

Although there are no exact rules to follow in goal setting, there are some principles which have been effective in the past for maximizing performance:

- ✈ Give the goal a definite end
- ✈ Set short and long term goals
- ✈ Set challenging but not overwhelming goals
- ✈ Evaluate performance instead of outcome
- ✈ Constantly reevaluate goals
- ✈ Create goals that lead to visible or measurable change

A "quiet determination to achieve" helps prevent conflict between opponents and teammates and usually furthers the competitive spirit. Successful skydiving competitors understand that the competition is not a fight between opponents but a struggle to realize personal and collective development.

In addition to inner forces driving competition, the social or physical environment plays a roll in furthering or inhibiting growth through competition. If a competition is disorganized, or the materials needed to compete are in short supply, competitors may be distracted and not perform at their best.

Desire may prompt plan development. Motivation may get one to the drop zone. A theory may help with navigation through plan realization. But if recreational pursuits take the place of training then the only goal one is moving toward is one of recreation. The old competitor saw, "What is not included in training does not suddenly appear in competition," applies as much to skydiving as any other sport.

WEATHER

Weather is one physical aspect of the skydiving environment trumping competition and everything else on a drop zone. When it plays its hand, parachute operations –training, competition, and recreation– bow before it. It decides who jumps, when, and to a large degree how. Natural forces can even dictate what kind of equipment jumpers use.

Of the many forces of nature, cloud cover deserves attention as one of the largest natural elements controlling whether or not airplanes fly and jumpers jump. Solid clouds overhead leave little doubt that skydiving will be delayed or limited. A solid layer of clouds push down the maximum attainable jump altitude, not only because it is impractical and unwise to jump through clouds, but also because it violates federal law. Jumpers flying over clouds cannot see the ground from the airplane, so cannot know where they are flying relative to their ideal exit point or the intended landing area. Worse, they can't see obstacles inside or below the clouds, or their thickness.

Probably the single largest reason for not jumping over clouds, and the reason the FAA is concerned with the practice, is that it introduces the possibility of a jumper-airplane collision. In reality jumper-aircraft collisions are exceptionally rare events. But the reason they are so terrible, and the reason the government forbids jumping during periods of limited visibility, is because a jumper colliding with an airplane endangers the airplane's unwitting occupants. They, after all, did not ask to participate in a skydive.

So jumping through solid clouds is out. How about making a jump below a solid cloud bank? That's O.K. as long as the cloud bottom is higher than the altitude needed for the desired jump. For example, if the bottom of the clouds lay at 4000' and the intent is to exit the airplane, deploy a parachute, and enjoy being a canopy pilot, then the jump may be made. If the intent is to make a 100 person formation in freefall then the jump will have to wait.

When cloud cover starts to break up and blue sky shines through, decisions of whether to jump or not to jump grow less concrete. Collective experience gained and codified also provides excellent advice on how much blue versus how much grey is O.K.. Trying to decide if the advantages of jumping outweigh the disadvantages of falling prey to the ravages of natural or federal law provide a rich source of anxiety for skydivers. Big, white, puffy clouds are beautiful and lend an awesome backdrop to any skydive, but too many too close together can make exiting over that ideal exit point and landing in that ideal area a daunting task.

The second major player in the weather game is wind. The sky can be crystal blue, but if the wind is blowing too fast jumpers may find it the better part of valor to stay on the ground and skydive another day. Our government is not concerned with the question of winds. The government is interested in protecting "the other guy" and sees wind speed as a factor only potentially harming the actor. Of course, if you happen to be that actor hanging over an obstacle or caught in frightening turbulence then you are intimately concerned with wind. How much wind is too much? Let's look again to cumulative wisdom for an answer.

For collective wind wisdom we turn to the US Parachute Association's, Skydiver's Information Manual. The SIM outlines reasonable wind speeds by subpopulation, but leaves a great deal of leeway for decision making. The main groups USPA offers wind recommendations for are unlicensed skydivers and skydivers using round reserve parachutes. The reason so many subpopulations are left out is because parachute center staff and individuals must be free to determine wind limits for their site or personal ability level.

Some sites have obstructions on the surrounding terrain which can cause the wind to tumble or otherwise interfere with its uniform movement over the ground. This disruption manifests as downdrafts, rotors, thermals, dustdevils, and whirligigs (a whirligig is a wind anomaly that doesn't fall into any other category). Taken together these interferences are called turbulence.

The effects of turbulence apply differently to different locales. Along the east coast there are drop zones with trees, hills, or buildings surrounding a small landing area. Some of these sites have found it necessary to extend the same guidelines used for unlicensed skydivers to all skydivers. Places in Florida, California and Hawaii regularly get strong winds, but have flat, obstruction-free terrain, so have higher wind tolerances. Modern parachutes are fast, but they are still pieces of fabric susceptible to nature.

Supporting actors in the weather game include cold and rain. Cold weather alone does not physically hamper skydiving. As long as the airplane will start and jumpers are willing to endure the temperature there is little to stop them. Indeed, jumps have been made onto the South Pole. The down side is that jumping in cold is uncomfortable and equipment doesn't perform as predictably in extreme cold as it does in more temperate climates. Some skydiving operations located in cold areas close down in winter, not because it is unsafe to operate, but because of a significant drop in business.

There are no federal or USPA guidelines for jumping in rain so long as cloud clearances are observed. It is uncomfortable though. A human body moving at human body speed quickly outpaces a raindrop moving at raindrop speed. A skydiver freefalling through rain can expect 1000 tiny needles pelting any exposed skin. Rain also gets equipment wet, a potentially disastrous condition for some of today's expensive, high-tech gear.

Turbulence

Turbulence, eddies, thermals, rotors, dirty air; it goes by many names, but the effect on a canopy's performance is the same. Turbulence disturbs the steady, clean air modern parachutes thrive in. It pushes on the top or bottom skin or robs the canopy of the rammed air keeping it inflated.

There are three guises turbulence takes to wreck havoc on an unsuspecting parachute. Windshear, thermals, and obstacle induced turbulence are as real a problem as buildings, power lines, or trees. Wind shear occurs when layers of air move at different speeds or in different directions. Heated, rising air generates thermals. Obstacles cause air to tumble, roll, and spin on the downwind side generating downward and upward bursts close together. What makes this downwind turbulence even more troublesome is that it usually attacks parachutes low to the ground where there is little room for recovery.

With ground winds less than 10 miles per hour, the downwind side of an obstruction can create eddies 10 to 50 feet in depth. Faster wind speeds or higher obstacles create greater turbulence. Even light winds pushed up mountainsides or down valleys can form major eddies with violent, abrupt characteristics. Aircraft or canopies in flight can generate a wake turbulence similar to downwind turbulence and disrupt aircraft following behind too closely. Turbulence can collapse a canopy at low altitudes, generate unexpected lift, and reduce expected lift.

Skydiving is supposed to be fun. Jumping in high winds, through clouds, in rain, or in extremes of temperature can move a day at the drop zone to a day at the hospital. That's no fun. It is far more prudent when weather is questionable or marginal to stay on the ground wishing to be in the air than to be in the air wishing to be on the ground.

Most of the problems associated with turbulence come from

jumping in winds that are too fast and can be prevented by staying on the ground when the wind picks up. In short, flying a parachute through masses of air moving at different speeds or in varying directions makes for a rough ride. To combat the effects of turbulence, skydivers should learn to read the wind and visualize its unseen movement. Watch other canopies. Check their penetration and observe how they fly at key altitudes. Look at upwind obstacles: trees, buildings, hills, and see the wind tumbling horizontally up to twenty times the height of the obstacle. Think about how your canopy would react if it got hit by some of that turbulent, "dirty," air.

Slowing a canopy 30% to 50% when accidently caught in turbulence will help stabilize it as it passes through. Less than 30% brakes allows the canopy to react more unexpectedly to turbulent air. More than 50% brakes slows the canopy to the verge of a stall and increases recovery time should a stall occur.

It is often tempting to jump when the sun is shining but the wind is blowing. You can see the landing area. You can convince yourself that if the exit point were carried just a little further upwind you would be able to make the airport. That might be true as long as there is a constant, unobstructed airflow to fly through. Too often though, it is not the simple wind speed which poses danger, but a difference in wind speeds and their respective angles of attack.

WHAT IS DANGEROUS ABOUT SKYDIVING?

"Skydiving? You skydive? That's very dangerous. What happens if your parachute doesn't open?"

This is a common reaction often spawned by ignorance. But generated by ignorance or not, the statement that skydiving is dangerous is true and valid. Participants can be, and are, injured and killed during the life cycle of a skydive. Skydiving is dangerous, often for reasons not even dreamed of, and sometimes not for reasons the uninitiated suspect.

Most people understand at some level that the sport is dangerous. But questioning frequently reveals little understanding of why it is dangerous or what exactly is dangerous about it. To build this understanding we must look at the skydiving population. Looking at a snapshot of the ultimate penalty for skydiving participation and who is represented there will furnish a better understanding of which subpopulations are more inclined to experience the heavy hand and fickle finger of skydiving's wrath.

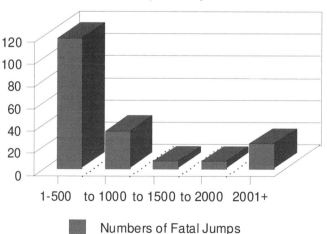

Fatalities by Experience

As can be seen from the graphic on the previous page, skydiving fatalities over a ten year period form a roller coaster-like curve. As might be expected, novice skydivers represent a large portion of these fatalities. As one gains experience the statistical probability of meeting one's demise on a skydive diminishes. From the 1000 jump mark until reaching the 2000 jump mark one can carry a statistical smiley face on every skydive. Then the graph jumps once more after the 2000 jump mark.

What might explain these two spikes? The first is undoubtedly due to a lack of experience or propensity to operate outside a personal performance envelope. It may also be true that the unsupervised novice is overwhelmed with the number of potential avenues to explore. Considering a spectrum of spectrums representing everything from what to buy to what to do may lead new skydivers into territory for which formal training could not begin to prepare. An eagerness to try out skills, develop new ones, and fit into the skydiving community may also play its card.

These theories and others point to a lack of understanding, ignorance, as a root fatality cause in the one to 1000 jump range. Modern formal training does a good job of imparting technical skills like canopy control, packing, and stability. Little training time is allotted in most curriculums for teaching new skydivers which equipment is appropriate, how and when to say "no" to peer pressure, or how to expand performance without tearing one's personal envelope. Whether or not a skydiving course could or should attempt to impart these attitudinal skills is driven, as is much of skydiving's method and machinery, by market demand, public opinion, and what filters down into the collective consciousness from those leading the sport's development.

If ignorance or overstepping limits describes fatalities in the 1 to 1000 jump range, what is it that the 1000 to 2000 jump group has learned which reduces its collective risk? Perhaps having survived the steep part of the learning curve they have developed more adaptive strategies and attitudes. It might be assumed that this group, having been exposed to skydiving longer than the less experienced group, has had time to learn which choices are appropriate for which skydiver. Possibly seeing the results of poor choices also enhances this awareness.

Armed with experience and proper equipment it would seem that fatalities would continue declining as experience increased. This is not the case. What might explain the second rise in fatalities for the 2100+ jump group? One word, complacency, can explain a sizable portion. Paul Sitter, keeper of U.S. skydiving fatality statistics for over fifteen years, cites complacency time and again as the culprit luring otherwise prudent and very competent skydivers astray.

A study of history supports this, teaching that almost anything novel, after a period of euphoria, loses its newness and becomes ordinary. Groups of people participating in edgy political or economic structures, educational hierarchies, or "extreme" sports gradually begin to accept ideas, sometimes sincerely bizarre ideas, as givens. Skydiving, while novel and exciting to the new skydiver, later slides into the normal and comes to rest in the realm of the routine.

Caught in this process of normalization, skydivers can be lulled into a sense of security not in keeping with the vigilance required. Complacent skydivers progressively take more for granted and let "small things" slip by. A distracted or complacent skydiver can fall prey to any of 1000 dangers not even considered to which an experienced AND alert jumper would not be subjected.

What can be done to reduce complacency? I can think of two things: continuing education and the cultural normalization of non-complacent practices across skydiving populations. This sport has learned much from skydivers in the upper experience echelons. Maybe all skydivers could learn something from those in the lowest fatality echelons.

Risk Assessment

We know that skydiving is dangerous. Developing plans for handling skydiving emergencies demands forethought, positioning, and a thorough understanding of equipment and environment. Equipment and landing problems accounted, according to Paul Sitter (*Parachutist*, May 98, '97 Fatality Summary), for 51% of 1997 US skydiving fatalities.

Approximately 125,000 people make at least one jump in the United States each year. While most make only one jump, the group logs around 2 million. Given that the average jump lasts eight minutes from preparing to exit the airplane to moving off the landing area, 125,000 jumpers making 2 million jumps are exposed to a total of 200,000 hours of "skydiving exposure" time per year. That breaks down to 16 hours of exposure time per person per year.

There have been an average of 37.6 skydiving related fatalities per year for the past twenty years. If each jump resulting in a fatality is considered a "hazardous" eight minute period, we find a five hour forty minute "hazard exposure period" in the 200,000 hour total time.

Five hours forty minutes is roughly .003% of 200,000 hours. One may then assume, in a *VERY* broad sense, that skydivers have a .003% (that's three hundreds of one percent) chance of meeting their demise on any given skydive. Every time we make a skydive we begin with a clean slate, statistically, and figuratively draw our lot. The reader must understand that these general observations cannot be taken as absolutes. As demonstrated, certain subgroups within the skydiving population are at greater risk, while others bear lesser risk.

Liability

Liability; the concept of personal responsibility for another's well being, can stir dark imaginings in almost any skydiver's mind. It should. Our civil system institutionalizes the idea that, while taking care of ourselves, we should not take unreasonable advantage of others. This system helps restore balance and acts as a deterrent to negligent or intentional acts of harassment. Without civil liability many devices, systems, and thought processes which increase our daily margin for error would not exist. There would be no seatbelts or airbags, police could routinely take extreme measures to selectively enforce laws, and housing would be fire-prone, asbestos–lined and covered in lead. Individual citizens could disavow contracts on a whim, making our economic machine struggle to operate.

What scares many people is the apparent unpredictability of civil cases. Decisions appear to go either way for no reason. But there are reasons for outcomes of civil cases. There are things drop zone operators, instructors, and Joe Skydiver can do to decrease the possibility of being sued, or if sued, sued successfully.

First, it is important to understand that case and statutory law vary widely from state to state, and that it is in a skydiver's best interest to familiarize his or her self with state-specific law. It may be difficult research but is necessary and worthwhile. "[Skydiving liability] is an area of the law that has not been fully litigated yet," says Liza Ross, a skydiver and Criminal Defense attorney practicing in San Diego, CA. Second, there are threads which connect these cases and statutes which may be woven into a model for drafting waivers, running a skydiving operation, or simply conducting oneself on the drop zone.

The skydiving liability model relies heavily on the assumption of personal responsibility. Drop zones use a waiver to formally define who is responsible for what. This instrument may be summarized in one word: reasonableness. "Reasonableness," asserts Bruce Throckmorton, an attorney practicing in New Jersey, "is the single most important aspect of a liability waiver." Courts across the country have upheld skydiving liability waivers time after time.

The assumption of personal risk is an important concept for skydivers to internalize. The waiver is a strong instrument institutionalizing this idea: *you* are the primary guarantor of your own safety.

What then makes a waiver reasonable? Many courts say that clear, common language, readable type, and bold warnings all add to the reasonableness of what is being asked. A waiver should make it very clear that skydiving is a dangerous activity and that participants could be injured or killed as a result of participation. The feat here is that while the language should be common and easily understood it should also detail the exact rights waived. As long as a waiver meets a court's concept of reasonableness even a failure to read it may not stand as a defense.

Cases supporting liability waivers:

Banfield v. Louis, 589 So.2d 441 (Fla. App. 1991)

Boyce v. West, 71 Wash. App. 657, 862 R2d 592 (1993)

Dombrowski v. City of Omar, 199 Mich,App. 705, 502 N.W. 2d 707 (1993)

Garrison v. Combined Fitness Center, Ltd., 201 Ill. App. 3d 581, 559 N.E.2d 187 (1990)

Hiett v. Lake Barcroft Community Association, 418 S.E. 2d 894 (Va. 1992)

Hoke v. San Diego School District, 274 Cal. Rptr. 647 (1990)

Jones v. Dressel, 623 P.2d 317 (Colo. 1981)

Liability Waivers and Releases Overview: Can you say 'exculpatory agreement?' National Recreation and Park Association Law Review

Scott v. Pacific West Mountain Resort, 834 p.2d 6 (Wash. 1992)

Section IV

Equipment

EQUIPPED FOR THE TRIP

Almost all sports hobbies or recreations require equipment. Some activities require little equipment for top performance. Skydiving is skill *and* equipment intensive. Generally, the better skydiving equipment one has, the less one must concentrate on gear and the more mental faculties can be devoted to skill improvement. But equipment that is "better" for one skydiver may be downright destructive for another. Equipment does not make the skydiver but can make skydiving easier or more difficult. As skills and interests develop so do needs for differing types of equipment.

Standard equipment for recreational skydivers includes two parachutes, a harness assembly, goggles, helmet, jumpsuit, and altimeter. Parachutes continue to get smaller, lighter, more reliable, and more comfortable to wear and use. Modern ram air parachutes are comparable with round parachutes only in the sense that they slow a descending object or person enough to land.

To understand the ram air design, imagine two rectangular pieces of material, one on top of the other and sewn together along the sides and the back, leaving the front open. Between these layers are sewn ribs which hold the upper and lower layers in a wing-like shape and divide the parachute into sections called "cells." Ram air parachutes are often described by their square footage and number of cells.

By the time one starts training with the intent to obtain a license, it is a good idea to accumulate some personal skydiving gear. Owning equipment, even if it's a cheap pair of goggles, provides a sense of independence and control not present when relying on community equipment. Having equipment offers one less potential drain of psychic energy or snag point for distraction. If, for example, you own your own goggles then you know they are adjusted and clean.

Helmet	Altimeter	Skydiver's Information Manual
Appropriate jumpsuit	Goggles	Logbook

ASAP Purchasable equipment

You should also be in the market for a complete rig (main parachute, reserve parachute, and container system). There are many equipment manufacturers, each with its own product lines and sizes. Consult the drop zone staff for suggestions on which type of gear they recommend. Scanning the Internet and looking through *Parachutist* or *Skydiving* magazines may provide good equipment leads as well. Many drop zones deal with one or more manufacturers and can assist with ordering.

Other useful items, like gloves and equipment bags, may be found in sporting goods stores. A copy of The Skydiver's Information Manual published by the U.S. Parachute Association is also a good purchase. It has vital information for passing license exams and performing specialized jumps.

The Parachute

Drag vs. Lift

The parachute, the aerodynamic decelerator, was conceived by DaVinci, tested by Andre' Garneran, and revolutionized by Jalbert. Since 1797 the parachute has been a means of lowering people and objects safely from a height. Firefighters, skydivers, paratroopers, bombs, food, mail, spacecraft, and supplies of all types have descended with the aid of the parachute. It has naturally had to evolve to accommodate these diverse needs. But nowhere has the parachute evolved so dramatically, or with such neck wrenching speed, as in skydiving.

Veterans returning from World War II formed parachute clubs using military surplus parachutes. Hard landings and a crippling lack of control coaxed some parachute pioneers to modify their canopies for greater control over the new environment they were exploring. These were simple modifications. They found that removing portions of material from the canopy permitted the parachutist to cut into the wind to a small degree. Attaching lines to these modifications allowed the parachutist to control canopy heading.

These sport parachutists eventually discovered that modifying existing designs could carry them only so far. They needed smaller, lighter, and more reliable equipment. Exiting paratroopers en masse over large tracts of land was fine for the bulky, uncontrollable military equipment. It would actually reduce safety for large numbers of people to be in the air at a very low altitude under high-performance canopies.

Yes. The round parachute and static line were fine for the military, but skydivers had decided the time had come to break from their military roots and follow their own way. This era of parachute experimentation, which incidently corresponded to the era of social experimentation in the '60's and '70's, saw many designs come and go. X-shaped parachutes, triangle shapes, and shredded looking shapes had their opportunity to address the size, weight, reliability, controllability, and landing concerns of skydivers.

The Para-Commander parachute survived to act as a thread and point of reference through this turbulent period. The Para-Commander, or PC, was lighter, packed smaller, and offered greater wind penetration than did modified military equipment. Even the landings were softer. An experienced parachutist could now land standing up. This parachute appeared to have been shredded by an overzealous parachute rigger, but in reality had been arduously designed and tested to deflect cupped air and maximize forward drive. It even came in colors other than olive drab, an option making it distinctly skydiving.

Though still at the height of its popularity, the year 1963 marked the beginning of the end for the Para-Commander. As kite maker Domina Jalbert gazed over an airplane's wing, daydreaming, he was struck by an epiphany which would change skydiving forever. He imagined a fabric wing and set to work on the ram air kite. The result was a fabric airfoil which looked like an airplane's wing minus the leading edge. Air entered the missing nose, was rammed into the sealed off tail, and inflated the structure. Internal ribs held upper and lower skins of the wing in Bernoulli's lift-producing, airfoil shape.

Based on, and some say stolen from, the original model by Jalbert, the ram air kite became a parachute. The ram air parachute received a patent in 1965, but it would still be ten or twelve years before it was widely accepted. Laughed at as a "flying mattress," the initial design suffered serious problems. It was not very reliable and opened so hard that it could only be used subterminally: just after exiting the plane.

A properly handled ram air parachute could be landed with the ease of stepping off an escalator. An improperly handled ram air parachute could cause significant grief for its pilot. At first it looked as though this would be just another fad parachute. But the speed with which it covered ground and its soft, flared landings beckoned some to work on the design.

Line lengths and packing methods were varied in efforts to improve reliability and performance. Devices were installed to slow down openings. And holes, called crossports, were cut in the internal ribs to balance air pressure. Designers eventually solved initial problems and ram air parachute sales began hedging out PC sales.

At one time a skydiver needed 500 round parachute jumps before transitioning to a ram air. Today, ram air canopies are standard at all USPA affiliated drop zones and are used by almost all active skydivers.

Ram air parachute use offered skydivers unique advantages. First, forward air speed and control dramatically improved. Square parachutes covered about three feet of ground for every foot of descent. Even early models had a 20 to 25 mile per hour forward speed. This meant that a parachutist was less at the mercy of the wind and could return to the landing area more easily from a poor exit spot. Second, the parachute could use this greater forward speed for additional lift during landing; in effect negating descent

134

rate and eliminating horizontal movement for extremely soft landings. Third, the parachute packed up smaller. This made the airplane ride more comfortable, but more important, it allowed more skydivers to exit closer together.

While its fundamental design has not changed since 1965, modifications to, and experimentation with, the simi-rigid wing has not stopped. Parachute manufacturers continue their efforts to provide modern skydivers with faster, more reliable, smaller packing, better landing parachutes. These efforts center around increasing the rigidity of the airfoil, reducing drag, increasing stability, and improving control. Skydivers are no longer passive passengers on a descent to earth at the mercy of the wind. They are pilots of low performance aircraft, flying their craft while plying their craft.

Parts of a Parachute System

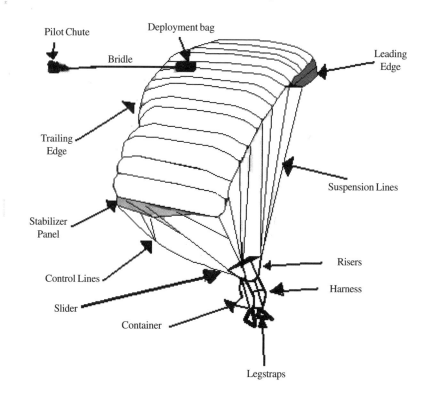

Main parachute

As its name implies, a parachute guards against (*para*) a fall (*chute*). Parachutes protect from falling in one of two ways: by increasing drag or producing lift.

Drag parachutes, called "round" parachutes, cup air to dramatically increase drag with the atmosphere. Once cupped, the air inside the parachute becomes potential energy and may be selectively spilled or deflected in order to change heading or slide horizontally during the descent.

Lift designed parachutes are fabric wings, like airplane wings with the leading edge missing. Air enters through the leading edge and is rammed into the closed tail. The parachute inflates and is kept inflated by air continuing to press into the leading edge while a fabric support structure holds the canopy in an airfoil, lift-producing shape. Because of this continuous ramming of air to maintain canopy inflation, lift producing canopies are called ram-air canopies.

Both drag and ram-air parachutes are used today for specialized applications. Time and experience have proven the ram-air design suitable for most skydiving purposes and positioned it as the centerpiece of skydiving paraphernalia. In trained and experienced hands a well maintained ram-air parachute opens reliably, offers a range of landing and performance options, and is maneuverable in ways a drag parachute cannot even pretend. In untrained or underprepared hands the ram-air parachute can be deadly.

Before continuing, there are a few parachute terms you should understand. A parachute's "cord" is its measurement from nose to tail (leading edge to trailing edge), while "span" is measured from side to side. An "angle of attack" is the angle of the nose relative to the tail. The nose, or leading edge, of the parachute is held lower than the tail to allow air to enter and fill the canopy. A sharp attack angle adds speed both forward and down while sacrificing horizontal distance. A parachute with a shallow angle offers improved glide ratio. Glide ratio or "glide path" describes how much a parachute flies forward when compared to how much it descends. A given parachute, for example, might be said to fly three feet forward to every foot of descent, or have a 3:1 glide ratio.

Attached to the bottom of the parachute platform are suspension lines used to carry the load and distribute it evenly through the canopy skeleton. Ram air canopies have four line groups identified from nose to tail as A, B, C, and D. A and B groups and C and D groups join below the bottom skin to form single line groups dubbed A and C. Suspension lines attach at their lower end to four thick straps called "risers."

Each of these four riser line groups run through a corner of a rectangular, reinforced piece of material called a slider. The slider separates the line groups, controls the lines during deployment, and slows the opening. Without a slider the parachute would open very fast, possibly damaging the equipment or its operator. Control lines, those lines used to steer the parachute, attach at their upper end to both sides of the canopy's tail and at their lower end to control toggles secured at the back of the risers. Finally, the risers attach to the harness with a riser release mechanism (see illustration on next page).

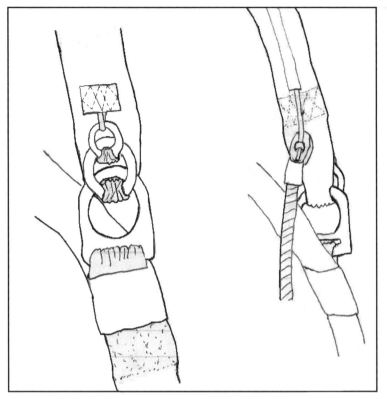

Riser Release Assembly

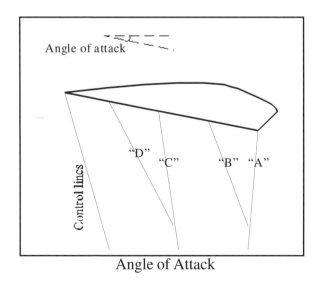

Angle of Attack

Most modern parachutes have seven or nine cells. Generally, seven-cell parachutes have a steeper glide ratio than nine celled models. This means, given otherwise identical conditions, that the nine cell will cover more ground horizontally while the seven cell can more easily sink steeply into a target area. Neither is better than the other. Each has its own applications. Sometimes it is better to cover more ground. At other times it is better to be able to come almost vertically down into a small landing area.

The amount of weight a given parachute carries dramatically affects its performance and is expressed as a weight to surface area ratio. This ratio is determined by dividing the exit weight of the jumper, including all equipment carried, with the surface area of the parachute jumped. For example, if a 190lb jumper (including equipment) were jumping a 240^2 ft. canopy ($190/240=.79$) he or she would be loading that parachute at .8:1.

As wing loadings increase (1:1, 1.2:1, 1.5:1 etc.), both forward speed and rate of descent proportionately increase. An advantage of a higher wing loading is improved speed for landing. A disadvantage to a higher wing loading is a decrease in the margin for error. Skydivers interested in high performance canopy flight should follow a logical progression and consult experienced canopy pilots (refer to section on induced-speed landings).

Reserve Parachute

The Federal Aviation Administration requires two parachutes be carried on all intentional parachute jumps. The FAA dictates how reserve parachutes are tested, how often they are inspected, and certifies people who do the inspecting and packing. Modern reserve parachutes are worn on the back above the main parachute in the container. Reserve parachutes are a skydiver's last chance. As such, it makes sense that they undergo stringent requirements for design, inspection, and packing. And while they are rarely used, procedures for their use lie at the core of skydiver training.

A skydiver does not normally see the contents of his reserve container. After packing, the reserve container is sealed to detect tampering and identify the rigger who packed it. A reserve parachute may be of any design as long as its manufacturer obtains a Technical Standard Order, or TSO, from the FAA. TSOing a reserve or harness requires drop testing, heat testing, cold testing, and pressure testing under varied conditions. Only after passing these tests may the reserve be manufactured and sold in the United States.

Reserve parachutes evolve like other skydiving equipment. But they do so at a slower rate due to the extensive testing required. Most modern reserves are square, ram air types. But many serviceable round reserves are still in use. Round parachutes have a place. Paratroops use the round. Most pilot emergency parachutes are round. Smoke jumpers use round parachutes. Round parachute use requires less training and offers a wide margin for operational error. With the exception of a few design variations intended to improve opening speed and reliability, ram air reserves operate identical to ram air mains.

Whether round or square, the reserve is a life saving device. It must submit to testing and inspection requirements not required of main parachutes. Learning when and how to use it is one of the first tasks new skydivers must master, and periodic practice in its use continues throughout the skydiver's career.

What to Look for when buying a Ram Air Parachute

Skydivers look first to wing loading when deciding which canopy to buy. Generally, the more experienced, confident, and competent the skydiver the higher wing loading he or she may seek. Of course experience, confidence, and competence are relative concepts, and even those who are experienced and confident may not desire a faster parachute.

Beyond wing loading, a person looking for a canopy might look at the number of cells. A nine cell parachute covers more ground from a given height than an identically loaded seven cell. Which one the skydiver chooses depends on what kind of skydiving he or she intends to pursue. Seven cell canopies are excellent for accuracy or demonstration skydives. They can get into tight landing areas more easily than fast flying nine cell models. Many canopy formation groups prefer seven cell parachutes; as do many camera flyers. On the other hand, nine cell canopies are excellent general purpose parachutes. They can better compensate for poor exit spots, drive into the wind better than seven cell canopies, and offer more lift for the landing flare.

Canopy size and number of cells are important, but so is fabric. F-111 fabric is Nylon, but not air tight and allows some amount of air to pass through. The amount of air passing through a parachute's skin is referred to as its permeability. As a canopy ages, permeability increases. Packing a parachute made from F-111 is somewhat less time consuming and aggravating than packing Zero Porosity fabric. Z-P is Nylon, but is far more resistant to the sun's effects than F-111, lasts longer, and retains its value longer.

Once a prospective parachute purchaser settles on wing loading, number of cells, and fabric, he or she may add extras. A given wing may be rectangle shaped, with an elliptical tail, or with both the nose and tail tapered on the sides. Elliptical canopies are more difficult to build than straight squares, so are usually more expensive. But they offer improved speed and lift for landing. Taper reduces the amount of dirty air, or vortices, swirling off the tips of the wing. Still another design option growing in popularity are air locks. These locks are sewn into the nose and allow air to enter but not escape. The result is a more rigid airfoil with less susceptibility to turbulence.

Finally, the parachute buyer should decide on color scheme. This is important if joining a team or buying a canopy to match a jumpsuit or container pattern. Custom colors do not usually cost extra but may increase the time it takes to receive an order. Some manufacturers offer to rush orders for an additional fee, but even this can take quite a while depending on the company, time of year, and backlog. One way to get a custom parachute in a short time is to go through a dealer. Dealers reserve manufacturing slots in anticipation of selling parachutes and can offer custom colors in a relatively short time. Some manufacturers only sell their product through their dealer network.

An alternative to waiting on a custom canopy is to buy one in stock. Manufacturers make parachutes even when no orders are pending and some dealers buy parachutes and hold them for the I-don't-care-what-color-it-is cases. When buying canopies and containers separately, bear in mind that only the canopy, suspension lines, and slider come with a canopy order. Almost everything else comes with the harness/container.

Buying a used canopy is also an option. Taking this route is just like buying a used car. Know and trust who is selling the parachute, have a reputable rigger inspect it, and try it for a few jumps before committing to buying.

Ultimately which parachute to buy depends on what the skydiver wants to do with it. Doing canopy relative work? Use a team compatible canopy loaded to a relative degree. Want to trade performance for ease of packing and cost? Choose F-111 instead of ZP. Just completed training and looking for a first parachute?

Get a docile, moderately loaded canopy. If buying used equipment ask an instructor for advice on who to buy from, jump it before buying, and have a rigger inspect it. Skydiving becomes more specialized, task-specific, and custom all the time. Buying a parachute is a daunting and difficult task for anyone, but there is a parachute right for each task and for each person performing that task.

Harness Container

Every skydiver wears a harness to which main and reserve parachutes attach. Each parachute packs into its own container until needed. Modern harnesses and containers are built as a single unit in the factory. Main and reserve parachute suspension lines attach to the harness via lengths of webbing, called risers. Main parachute risers connect to the harness at the shoulders with a release system. Reserve parachutes connect to independent and non-releasable risers.

The main harness webbing supporting a jumper is called the main lift web. Leg straps fix to the lower end of the main lift web and form adjustable loops for the legs. An adjustable piece of webbing secured across the chest is the chest strap which prevents the parachutist from falling forward between the lift webs. Straps across the back keep the jumper from falling backward. A harness manufacturer, like a reserve manufacturer, must satisfy the government (FAA) of its product's airworthiness before selling it.

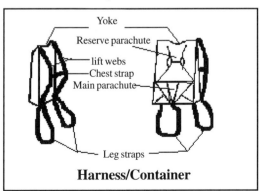

Harness/Container

A container attached to the harness holds both main and reserve parachutes until one or the other is needed. Today, harnesses and containers are fused into a single unit and characterized by outside appearance or manufacturer label. One noteworthy feature distinguishing harness/ container systems, or simply "container" systems, are the design and number of flaps covering the reserve pilot chute. Some reserve pilot chutes are completely enclosed, some have one or two flaps covering them, and some are completely free of covering flaps. The main parachute packs below the reserve, and when both parachutes are packed, the main and reserve containers appear as seamless unit.

Buying a container is as bewildering an experience as buying a parachute. Novice skydivers looking for their first parachute system should turn to an instructor for advice. Calling manufacturers or suppliers and asking about their products is also a wise move.

Ensure that the container is not too large or small for the canopies it will contain. A container that is too large allows packed parachutes to shift around inside. A container that is too small will not close properly. The size of the harness is another point of concern. If a harness is too long or too short, parachute containers will not rest snugly against the back and the parachutist may not ride well under an inflated parachute. Ask an instructor where the emergency handles should rest, where the chest strap should lie, and where the junction of legstraps and main lift webs should sit against the hips.

Jumpsuits

A jumpsuit should be one of the first accessories a new skydiver buys. Jumpsuits cover clothes that could otherwise fill with air and cause difficulties in freefall, cover a handle, or flap against exposed skin. They help compensate for fall rate differences between jumpers and protect skin from those not-so-graceful landings.

The speed a skydiver falls is determined by a balance of surface area and air density to gravity and weight. We will cover that in greater detail later. For now understand that we can't adjust gravity or air density but can control weight or area of resistance to increase or decrease fall rate. A proper jumpsuit goes a long way in helping skydivers control drag variables in freefall.

Specialty jumpsuits, like specialty parachutes, make certain types of skydiving easier. Camera suits, for example, have large wings sewn under the arms to help camera flyers rapidly control fall rate and move around the sky. Sit suits have tight leggings and cups sewn under the arms to improve ability to sit in freefall. Some suits are baggy to slow down fast fallers. Some suits are tight to speed up lightweights. Each suit has its own application. And like parachutes and containers, each manufacturer has its own approach to that application.

A jumpsuit, like so much skydiving gear, is custom: custom fit, custom colors, custom options. Jumpsuit designers build suits with an understanding of how drag affects skydivers in freefall. This knowledge, coupled with high quality manufacturing, results in a smooth-flying suit that endures the stresses common to all skydiving equipment.

The "right" suit for you depends on your body composition, primary skydiving activities, and taste. Think about how fast you fall relative to those you regularly jump with. If you consistently have difficulty getting down to a group, a slicker, tighter-fitting suit is needed to reduce drag. If you consistently find yourself below the group, you need to add the drag of a loose fitting, cotton-type suit. Refer to the discussion of fall rate on page 78 for more detail.

To simplify buying, jumpsuits may be ordered in standard sizes. This eliminates the need to obtain measurements. For a more exact fit, wear the clothes you normally jump in and have someone measure you according to the manufacturer's guidelines.

A custom fit does not normally cost extra, but takes more time to build.

In addition to fit and drag concerns, the jumpsuit shopper must select a color scheme and options. Select colors that match other equipment, other skydivers, or your taste. Zippers on the leg, booties, extra grippers, reinforcing, a lining, wings, air cups, swoop cords and combinations of fabrics are options adding versatility, durability, and utility to a jumpsuit. Ordering a jumpsuit is a difficult process. But a need for the right tool has installed jumpsuit ordering as a skydiver rite of passage. Knowing what kind of skydiving a given suit is intended for goes a long way when ordering.

Peripherals

The harness/container system, a main parachute, and a reserve parachute form the bare essentials necessary to jump from an airplane. Beyond these basics are some *almost*-essential items and an endless supply of nice-to-have goodies.

Almost-Essential Items

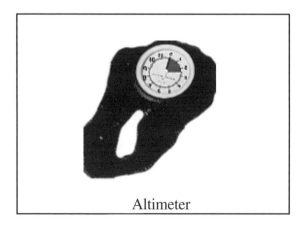

Altimeter

One key piece of peripheral equipment is an altimeter. The altimeter detects changes in air pressure and uses those differences to indicate altitude above the ground. Altitude awareness is essential for successful skydiving, and altimeters visually display altitude and promote altitude awareness. They back up a skydiver's finely honed perception of time and height above the ground. There are also devices to back up the back up.

One such device is the Automatic Activation Device, or AAD. AADs have become a popular addition to personal parachute assemblies. The AAD attaches to the reserve parachute, and when turned on and calibrated, calculates the speed and altitude of a descending skydiver. The AAD asks itself (electronically or mechanically) if the speed at the preset altitude is acceptable or unacceptable for landing. If the device's calibration tells it the rate of decent is not survivable then it releases the reserve pilot chute.

There are number of AADs on the market, each with its own marketing points and reliability level. A reliable AAD is an excellent addition to any skydiving setup, but is not a magic amulet to protect the skydiver from all harm. It should be noted that no safety device can take the place of awareness, training, increased margin for error, confidence, competence, or currency. Improper canopy control, disregard for aircraft propellers, or faulty emergency procedures will kill and maim just as surly as hitting the ground without an open parachute.

Reserve static lines, RSLs, are back up devices aiding proper emergency procedures. Like AADs, RSLs are required equipment for skydivers under supervision but optional for licensed skydivers. And like the AAD, the RSL is merely a backup to a manual reserve ripcord pull and not a substitute for proper training or practice.

A helmet in skydiving protects the head from bumps and thumps during rehearsals, in the airplane, in freefall, and on landing. Some helmets cover the ears or even the whole face to protect against cold and noise. Specialized helmets are used to mount cameras for hands free filming.

Skydiving goggles keep wind out of the eyes. Locating others in freefall or even reading an altimeter becomes difficult to impossible with eyes watering and vision blurring in a 120mph wind. Good goggles completely cover and seal the eyes but do not fog or obstruct peripheral vision. Goggles interfering with peripheral vision may restrict one's ability to see other skydivers or emergency handles under stress.

Peripheral vision aside, eye contact is an important factor to consider when buying goggles. Many types of skydiving work better when there is eye to eye contact between participants. Tinted and other goggle types may inhibit eye to eye communication.

The Military and Parachutes

Gearing up for a military jump

In the military the parachute is a means to an end, the objective being to get troops on the ground as quickly as possible so they can do something else. In skydiving, the parachute is an end unto itself. The activity serves as its own validation. While both military parachuting and skydiving share the parachute as a way to land people on the ground, that's where similarities end.

Military and civilian exit and deployment altitudes differ significantly. Parachute operation is different. Emergency procedures are different. Landings are different. Exit procedures are different. In short, military parachuting, even military freefall parachuting, is so different from skydiving that the two are almost incomparable. The objectives of each demand specialized techniques and equipment.

Getting troops on the ground while minimizing exposure to hostile fire calls for exiting from low altitudes using round parachutes. One might imagine the complications 64 paratroops could face zooming around the sky at twenty miles an hour after exiting from 800' and at night.

Paratroops are trained to jump by their branch of service. Military jump school lasts three weeks and is broken into three phases:

ground, tower, and jump week. During ground week, parachutist candidates work on physical fitness, exits, and landings. Tower week combines intensified fitness and technical practice with emergency procedure practice. The last week, jump week, combines all previous practice while introducing personal rigging procedures and making five qualifying jumps. After the fifth parachute landing the parachutist receives the coveted Airborne wings.

Military freefall parachuting is somewhat closer to skydiving than mass static line activities, but still differs dramatically in purpose and technique. Like skydivers, Military Freefall (MFF) parachutists use ram air parachutes to get to the ground. But MFF jumps are made from extremely high altitudes. The idea is to fly airplanes above hostile radar while low signature jumpers fall below detection. In High Altitude Low Opening operations, troops exit from 20,000' - 30,000' and freefall to around 4,000'. In High Altitude High Opening operations, jumpers exit and deploy high, then fly their parachutes cross country. All four branches of the armed forces use MFF troops.

The military promotes sport jumping by sponsoring recreational skydiving activities on its bases and supporting military teams. In doing so the service provides a meaningful recreation for its members, the sport gains skydivers, and the service member skydiver learns and practices economically. Service sponsored teams promote interest in the service and base they represent. The Golden Knights are an example of one such team and are the U.S. Army's full time parachute team.

The armed forces and sport parachuting have shared training, equipment designs, and human resources. Even so, the application and objectives of military and civil parachuting remain poles apart.

BASE Jumping

BASE is an acronym standing for "Building," "Antennae," "Span," and "Earth," and represents those objects fixed object jumpers jump from. Jumping from fixed objects is considered by some to be done by renegades and law breakers. The activity is not in itself illegal, but its application sometimes requires trespassing or vandalism. Most bridges and earthen structures large enough to jump from are on federal or state property. Most buildings and antennae are owned by people unwilling to accept liability should a jumper get injured on their property. Authorities have shown a zealous desire to apprehend BASE jumpers, fine them, and seize their gear. Still, there is organized movement toward establishing and promoting responsible BASE jumping.

Like skydiving, BASE is not for everyone. Aspiring BASE jumpers should never attempt jumping from a fixed object without consulting experienced practitioners. Each jumper should realistically evaluate his or her own performance envelope and be personally willing to accept BASE's inherent risks. Trying to impress someone or prove something is not a mature or constructive reason for BASE jumping or skydiving.

Additionally, every BASE jumper should first be a skydiver. There is simply no substitute for familiarity with equipment and how it performs under varied conditions. BASE is even more equipment intensive than skydiving. Being in good physical condition also helps, as fixed object jumping involves climbing and the landings frequently offer choices between the lesser of evils.

BASE jumps, by design, start out very low, 300'-800' in many cases. They also start from a motionless position. There is little airspeed to create drag for deploying a parachute. Airspeed, critical for timely parachute deployment, comes from jumping and delaying deployment of a single parachute. BASE enthusiast Walt Appel has written on equipment and training for fixed object jumps. Here are some things he considers important:

Deployment System- Each site is different. The deployment system (static line, pilot chute) is based on the length of freefall and the distance in which one needs an open canopy.

Canopy- Oversized canopies are a good idea. BASE landing areas are often very tight and offer difficult approaches. A large canopy will land softly under most conditions. The canopy is either packed without a slider installed, or with a modified slider.

Container System- Skydiving harness/container systems are suitable for some BASE jumps, but there are systems on the market designed specifically for jumping from fixed objects. These containers are the result of a great deal of research and experimentation.

Protective Gear- Wearing a helmet when BASE jumping is a good idea. Hard shell knee and elbow pads are a must. Wear footwear suitable for the landing area.

BASE jumping has come far from its humble beginnings and grown into its own. Like military parachuting and skydiving, BASE has both borrowed and lent technique and equipment design. There is still a long way to go. Improved organization and equipment and better media exposure continue to push BASE jumping out of the dark corners and into the light.

AROUND THE DROP ZONE

The national organization overseeing skydiving in the United States is the United States Parachute Association. USPA is a nonprofit organization in which each member may vote for a board of directors who help shape skydiving's development. The board is responsible for issuing directives and making policy that "keep skydivers skydiving." In pursuit of this goal, USPA has compiled and published information and established safety guidelines representing collective, accumulated skydiving wisdom.

To improve standardization and safety, USPA certifies instructors and administers the licensing system. The Association publishes a monthly magazine covering product, safety, and political issues. But perhaps the most important reason for joining USPA is that the organization has been instrumental in maintaining skydiver control of skydiving. Skydiving is currently one of the safest aviation sports and enjoys the least amount of federal regulation. To keep it this way it is important that skydivers police themselves.

USPA categorizes skydivers into six experience levels:

1. Students ▲ under direct supervision in a formal training program
2. Novices ▲ graduated from a student program but not yet licensed
3. A license ▲ minimum of 20 freefall jumps
4. B license ▲ minimum of 50 freefall jumps
5. C license ▲ minimum of 100 freefall jumps
6. D license ▲ minimum of 200 freefall jumps

USPA's representative on every member drop zone is the Safety and Training Advisor. S&TAs serve to verify license skill requirements. A license acts as proof of one's minimum ability levels. It is especially important for skydivers visiting drop zones away from their training site to have a license. Each license has its own currency requirements. Staying current (jumping regularly) is one of the most important things one can do to enhance personal safety. If you are away from skydiving for several weeks you will need to do some reviewing and get back into the sport with a simple, safe, supervised skydive.

USPA also issues instructional ratings to qualified applicants. A person holding a Coach rating has demonstrated skill necessary to guide novices through a post-training program. Instructors have attended instructor training courses. Either a coach or instructor will be able to answer most questions. New skydivers meet plenty of people willing to offer suggestions, but not every suggestion should be followed blindly.

Someone with one or two hundred jumps may seem very experienced to someone with ten jumps, but is actually a relative newcomer to the sport. One may occasionally hear experienced jumpers discussing techniques or procedures that differ from the standard training curriculum. Be aware that some things which may be safe for experienced jumpers could be inappropriate for novices.

Drop zone etiquette is open and casual, but when you are in an area where people are packing be sure to walk around their parachutes. Never smoke or leave drinks around parachute gear. Do not borrow or examine gear without permission. And drinking alcohol on the drop zone during jumping hours is forbidden and a rule extending to non-skydiving guests.

A Skill-Development Model (Or How to Grow Without Getting Hurt)

A skydiver's working skill set may be viewed as a personal performance envelope. Inside this envelope reside all skills meeting three criteria. First, every skill in the envelope must be doable every time under ideal circumstances. Second, every skill must be doable almost every time under challenging conditions. Third, every skill must be available a majority of the time under difficult conditions.

Any skill or skill set not meeting these conditions should be considered as outside the envelope and not relied on as a tool for learning or completing goals. Instead, desired skills residing outside the envelope may stand as goals to be worked toward. As an example, a novice skydiver has in his envelope a survival package. He understands the difference between stable and unstable bodies and canopies. He can consistently land a parachute in the landing area on a pretty day with a light breeze. He has received excellent, realistic training for aircraft, freefall, equipment, and landing contingencies which he frequently reviews. And he has made some progress with relative flight.

Now he wants to learn to sit in freefall. This skill lies outside his envelope, so he asks someone who knows. He might read a book on sit flying or ask a local sit flyer questions. "What do I need to do to sit fly? What equipment do I need? What modifications do I need to my present setup? What kind of exit is most effective? Will I burn up freefall time faster or slower in a sit?"

The aspiring sit flyer may then plan a simple, bare-bones sit fly skydive, possibly even jumping with the expert (now coach), while leaning on his current working skill set and drawing feedback from the coach. After making a number of jumps like this, trying one or two new things each time, the new sit flyer will have pulled in a few skills that had previously been outside the envelope.

Those skills inside the envelope represent competencies. Psychologists use the model below to describe progressive skill acquisition and competence building. Every skill in one's performance envelope must pass through each stage however swiftly or slowly.

STAGES OF COMPETENCE DEVELOPMENT

UNCONSCIOUS INCOMPETENCE: BEING UNABLE TO PERFORM A SKILL *AND* BEING UNAWARE OF THE INABILITY

CONSCIOUS INCOMPETENCE: BEING AWARE OF AN INABILITY TO PERFORM A SKILL

CONSCIOUS COMPETENCE: BEING ABLE TO PERFORM A SKILL WHILE ACTIVELY CONCENTRATING

UNCONSCIOUS COMPETENCE: BEING ABLE TO PERFORM A SKILL WITHOUT ACTIVE CONCENTRATION

In the first stage, unconscious incompetence, one is completely unaware of what is required. "Race car driving?" the unconscious incompetent might say, "I can do that! Just go fast and turn left."

In the second stage, conscious incompetence, the actor becomes aware of how little is known and is faced with a decision point. The conscious incompetent might say, "Electrical engineering sounds difficult, but I feel my heart and interests pulling me in that direction and am ready to commit myself to learning." On the other hand, the prospective electrical engineer, upon reaching the second stage, might say, "Whew! I didn't know there was so much math involved. I was initially excited about electrical engineering, but now I don't think I'm really interested."

It is in the third stage of skill development that the work of learning takes place. The conscious competent intentionally makes himself or herself uncomfortable exploring, not just the middle of the bell curve, but the tails also. A conscious competent learning to drive a car might say, "Ok, I'm going to pass this car. I need to check the passing lane, signal, change lanes, accelerate, confirm passage, signal, change lanes." The skydiver with skills in this stage studies and researches, asks questions and ponders, and practices, practices, practices. Actions in the third stage are often stilted and mechanical; sometimes spastic. But with enough practice each comes to dwell in the envelope.

Many skill sets remain permanent residents of the third stage. Some skills in this stage, those used the most, begin taking on a life of their own and begin to function independent of conscious thought processes. The unconsciously competent race car driver actually will go fast and turn left, even though his conscious thoughts are not on the mechanics of steering and acceleration, but on strategy and positioning. The fourth stage electrical engineer can design a circuit board while only visualizing the desired result. The car driver in this stage passes the slow poke while carrying on a conversation and may not even be consciously aware of the pass.

The unconsciously competent skydiver touches handles while walking to the plane without consciously thinking and constantly plans and replans a landing approach during parachute descent while consciously looking for other parachutists. A skydiver in the fourth stage may be overheard saying, "Man, we were crankin'! How many points did we turn? Let's look at that video!"

By now you understand that while skydiving you must be aware of several things: altitude, your own body position, your position relative to the ground, and your position relative to others. Initially this will seem like a lot to be aware of, so on your first few jumps you will concentrate almost entirely on altitude, body position, and canopy control while your instructors take care of the rest. When you are released to fly free, you will control your own heading. Eventually you will be able to monitor and control heading, formation center point, and line of flight as easily as you monitor speed, direction, location, and other traffic while driving your car to the drop zone.

Parachute Rigging

<u>Basic Packing</u>

At some point in the training process, drop zone staff introduces students to packing. Parachute packing is normally taught in two phases. First a classroom session covers theory, offers a demonstration, and provides intensive supervision. Later packing practice is done under staff supervision until students are able to pack on their own. Each parachute system differs slightly and procedures must be learned for each configuration. Do not guess! Packing a parachute does not require an advanced degree, but it does require concentration, focus, and an ability to follow proven guidelines. Ask an instructor about unfamiliar terms below.

<u>Packing Tips:</u>

√ Keep control lines and D-lines, together at the tail
√ Keep tension pulled on the lines up toward the canopy at all
      times while keeping the risers even
√ Stow the brakes (untwist the brake lines)
√ Check for frayed lines or lines getting ready to break
√ Cock the pilot chute
√ Uncollapse the slider
√ Pack the slider at the top of the lines (cloverleaf)
√ Clear the stabilizers and bridle to prevent canopy damage
√ Keep line stows tight (no stow should unstow before its time)
√ Know how to close the container (or find out)

<u>Equipment Inspection During Packing</u>

√ Check Velcro and Spandex for wear
√ Check closing loops (main and reserve) for fraying
√ Check for broken stitching in the harness
√ Lines wear at the links- check them there
√ Check slider grommets for sharp edges or damage
√ Ensure that the pilot chute handle is secure
√ Check that pilot chute material is crisp and the seams are intact

<u>Equipment Inspection During Packing continued</u>

√ Stitching for pin attachment to bridle is secure
√ Stitches on deployment bag stow band loops are not raveled
√ Bridle attachment point on top of canopy is secure
√ Stitching present on line attachment points
√ Slider installed with fabric side down
√ No corrosion or cracks on connector links
√ Connector links tight (finger tight + 1/4 turn)
√ No rust on rings or other riser hardware
√ No corrosion on brake line keeper ring
√ Toggles properly knotted
√ Cut away cables are clean (hard housings)

Stowing the lines

The Pre-flight

Flight Plan and Safety Check

Height_____Weight_____
Canopy Size_____ Wing loading _____:1

3-rings: In Order, Release Cable through Loop, RSL Fastened
    to Proper Ring

3-straps: In Good Repair, Threaded Properly
    Handles: Unrestricted Movement, Acceptable Pull
    Tension, Proper Location

Pilot Chute/ Ripcord: Acceptable Pull Tension, Properly in
    Pouch

Reserve Container: Closing Loop in New Condition, Closing
    Pin Satisfactorily Through Loop, AAD Set, Tuck Tabs
    in Place

Main Container: Closing Loop in Good Condition, Closing
    Pin/Cable Properly Routed, No Exposed Canopy, Pin
    Protective Flap Closed

Accessories: Altimeter- Set to Zero, Radio- Channel and
    Volume Test, Helmet- Proper Fit, Goggles- Clean &
    Snug, Gloves- Snug Fit (as needed), Jumpsuit- Appro-
    priate Size, Weight Vest- As Needed

Pockets Empty, Jewelry Removed, Shoes Tied, Collars Tucked,
Dressed for Temperature, Skydive Planned and Rehearsed

Skydive Plan

Type Skydive_____ Opening Altitude_____

Aircraft_____ Exit Type_____

Exit Altitude_____

Performance Points/ Sequence of Events

_____

_____

_____

Canopy Control Safety

√ Never land the ram-air canopy in a turn
√ After flaring for landing never return the toggles to the full-flight position
√ If you are too high or too far down wind when you turn to face the wind you will overshoot the landing area
√ If you are too low or too close to the target when you turn into the wind you will undershoot the landing area
√ Always keep plenty of clear area in front after turning to face the wind for landing
√ Always plan for alternate landing areas and keep your options open

Safety Summary

1. Reserve parachutes worn for skydiving must be in date. That means an inspection by a FAA rigger must have been performed within the preceding 120 days.

2. Seatbelts are worn during takeoff and landing by everyone on the aircraft.

3. Skydives are made, at a minimum, 1000' above any clouds, 500 feet below any clouds, and 2000 feet horizontal to any clouds.

4. Check that all equipment used is in good working order. Be sure the cut away cable housing is free of dirt and the cable extracts easily. Check the Velcro for wear. Check the lines for wear and stitching. Check the canopy for holes, stress runs, and debris. Check the connector links for tightness. These are all things that can be done during packing and the final equipment check.

5. When engaging in Formation Skydiving, preplan the breakoff altitude.

6. Always check main and reserve parachute pin seatings and bridle routing before boarding an airplane.

7. If wearing an AAD, check that it is armed before getting on the aircraft.

8. Check wind direction and speed before making a skydive. Plan where you are going to land and the landing direction.

9. Always be sure the pilot is briefed as to jump altitude, number of jumpers on board, and the number of passes.

10. All jumpers must sit where the pilot tells them to sit. This keeps the center of gravity as close to the wings as possible, making for a much safer takeoff.

11. Keep movement in the airplane to a minimum. This helps the pilot maintain a good rate of climb and a good center of gravity.

12. If there is a parachute deployment in the airplane try to contain the loose canopy and close the door.

Should any part of the canopy get out the door then the person wearing the system must leave immediately.

13. Always wave off and check the air above before deploying a parachute. This is a good habit even when jumping solo.

14. Minimum decision altitude for a cutaway is made by 1800 feet and initiated by 1600 feet.

Developing the Habit

Safety is a habit. Get in the habit of performing good pre-flight checks on your equipment before each and every jump. With practice, this pre-flight takes literally seconds to perform.

The main parachute should be checked for closing loop serviceability and proper pin seating. If the container is opened with an external pilot chute then the bridle routing should also be checked. Inspect the overall appearance of the main container. Are lines sticking out? Are the risers pulled down equally into the container? Is the pack noticeably bulky, loose, or distended? If it is, why?

The flap covering the reserve parachute pin should be opened and the reserve pin, AAD, and RSL inspected. The reserve pin is seated all the way through the closing loop and covered by a protective flap. AADs, regardless of model, should be checked for engagement and calibration. A reserve static line is connected at one end to the risers and at the other to the reserve ripcord. The reserve packing data card should also be checked to ensure that the last inspection was within 120 days (4 months).

At terminal velocity you pass through one thousand feet every six seconds. If you did not open your parachute, you would have a life expectancy of about 27 seconds from 4500'. Opening altitudes are assigned to allow skydivers sufficient time to correct problems and land under an open parachute- main or reserve.

When inspecting the harness, begin at the top and work down the front. Check the riser release assembly. The small ring goes through the middle ring, the middle ring goes through the large ring, and the loop goes over only the small ring. The loop routes through the grommet on the riser then through the cable housing grommet, and the cable passes through the loop.

Check the main lift webs. Ensure that the reserve ripcord and main parachute release handle (if applicable) is properly stowed. Check the leg straps for proper threading.

After donning the equipment make sure the leg straps are snug and even. Make sure the chest strap is properly routed. And make sure you can see and reach the emergency handles.

The Boogie

A boogie is a large gathering of skydivers or special skydiving event. It usually includes unusual or attractive jump planes and extensive after-dark partying. Some skydivers plan their annual vacation around skydiving boogies and some planes fly a "boogie circuit" from drop zone to drop zone.

Attending a boogie is one of skydiving's finer experiences. Mingling, talking, planning, and learning with other skydivers helps mix the broth of one's experience. But there are things to be on the look out for. Boogies attract large groups of inexperienced and uncurrent skydivers jumping unfamiliar airplanes and using unfamiliar equipment. With so many variables, the prudent skydiver plans for the "other guy." He or she looks out for spastic canopy control and doesn't lock in on landing where everyone else is landing. The alert skydiver at a boogie avoids things like inexperienced jumpers trying to build large formations.

Event organizers help unravel the tangled web of potential boogie problems. Always be up front and honest with them about experience and currency and never be afraid to say "No."

Space and Time

We've discussed the body's relation to the wind. Now let's look more closely at its relationship to space and time. When you leave an airplane at, say, 13,500 feet above the ground, you accelerate from zero miles per hour vertical speed to approximately one hundred and twenty miles an hour in about ten seconds. The acceleration effect, or roller coaster feeling, one might expect is substantially reduced since the aircraft's forward speed is already close to 100 miles an hour. So you are really only gaining about twenty miles per hour. At that point you reach terminal velocity. Ignoring minor body position changes you will stay at that speed until something stops you; hopefully parachute deployment.

Prior to Galileo, people believed that objects falling freely attained an instant terminal velocity dependent on their weight. After some experimentation this famous astronomer concluded that it was air resistance which changed an object's fall rate. The larger the object the slower it fell. The Apollo astronauts supported this finding when they dropped different sized objects (a wrench and a feather) from the same height in the vacuum of space (on the surface of the moon) and both fell at the same rate. This acceleration from a height is unique to gravity and was one inspiration for Einstein's General Theory of Relativity.

Galileo also showed that not only do objects accelerate, but that they do so uniformly. There are no sudden accelerations or jumps in speed. He found that for each second of fall a body travels the distance from the previous second plus 32.16 feet.

Much of skydiving physics centers on direction of movement, friction, and speed. Newton showed that once a body started moving that it tended to stay moving in one direction until acted on by a force. Einstein noted that in order to discuss Newton's force and motion effectively an observer had to be defined. All motion must be described relative to that observer. He also showed that movement was not arbitrary or static, but dynamic and relative.

At the moment of exit several relevant physical conditions exist. When the skydiver exits the plane, he or she is falling (forward and down) the same speed the plane is flying. We might say that the skydiver's initial speed is equal to the airplane's airspeed. As we accelerate, air friction comes increasingly into play. Four key variables are now on the table (or rather up in the air). They are atmospheric pressure (ap), velocity (v), surface area (s), and the drag coefficient (d). The formula looks like this: air resistance = ½(ap)(v)(v)(s)(d).

If you run the numbers you will be able to plot a graph showing acceleration up to the point that drag balances with air pressure. This is not a linear graph. Instead it looks like the one below.

Not only can we plot speed, distance, and resistance but we can also determine the force generated by acceleration. This force is expressed in Newtons and is derived by multiplying one's mass by the acceleration (F=ma). On the ground our acceleration due to gravity is 32.15 f/s. When a skydiver is at terminal velocity, force equals 0 Newtons.

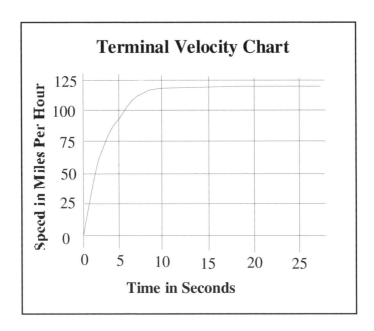

While skydivers have historically questioned the rules of man, all skydivers must submit to the physical rules of nature. There is forward throw of the airplane, there is atmospheric resistance, there is variable drag dependent on the body's presentation. There are other, more intangible variables, some of which involve human psychology and body composition, that further complicate the equation. Skydivers should have an understanding of skydiving science, but should balance and complement that understanding with an appreciation for the beauty and mystery of jumping from a perfectly good airplane.

Newton, Einstein, Gallileo and others created models that are useful in measuring, observing, and physically describing skydiving. But to know only that skydiver A is falling at X speed at Y point and has covered Z distance from the airplane does not convey the experience.

Methods for controlling stress

Maximizing skydive performance hinges on skydivers having the right tools and levels of environmental comfort. It also depends on moving thoughts in a constructive direction. The body follows the mind in the direction of its most dominate thought. Trafficking with thoughts of pain or failure will lead one, if not to pain or failure, then to dissatisfaction or the perception of failure. The secret to directing thoughts constructively lies in the willful wording of positive expressions. Successful skydivers start moving toward a goal by positively visualizing a concrete result. "Oh! I might break my leg," becomes, "I know how to land a parachute." "My parachute may not open," becomes, "I can read an altimeter, deploy stable, and apply emergency procedures if I need to."

Having a definite end to the task helps further reduce resource sapping stress. Large, open ended tasks lead to dark imaginings. "Packing parachutes looks so complicated. How will I ever learn to do it?" offers an example of thinking in open ended terms. Breaking any large task down into smaller units makes it much more manageable. "Ok. First I need to straighten the canopy and lines. That's easy enough. I can do that," represents a good first step and is not as overwhelming as trying to tackle the whole process of packing at once. Each step should be realistic and follow some logical order.

Reviewing the sequence of events further reduces anxiety levels. Physically practice and visualize all tasks leading to the realization of the goal. Yet, even with a good plan, preparation and the mind moving toward a concrete, manageable goal, the body can still inhibit performance.

Breathing and heartbeat increase when the body gets aroused. Realizing that behavior affects performance we can see how controlling behavior can help control performance. An effective but long-term method of controlling arousal is called desensitization. By taking baby steps to move closer to an anxiety-producer, aversive physical reactions may be controlled.

Some skydivers merely need to concentrate to control performance-sapping stress. We live in a culture built on distractions. Focusing on the task at hand, and only the task at hand, can greatly reduce extraneous distractions and improve perfomance. If breathing and heart rate continue to disrupt performance try breathing deeply and letting it out slowly. Consciously relax the jaw, neck, and shoulders where tension accumulates. Repeat this process several times while thinking only about the breathing.

Concentration improves with time and practice. In skydiving, concentration takes the form of relaxed alertness, and may be visualized as a cone within a cone. The inner cone of concentration focuses only on the task at hand while the outer cone absorbs and filters distraction.

A focused- relaxed state doesn't come from concentrating on concentration any more than it comes from concentrating on relaxation. Concentrating on concentration expends energy and reduces performance. Flow gets broken. The degree of concentration should ebb and flow with the demands of the skydive.

Performance is an outward reflection of one's inner ability to concentrate. An ability to focus on the correct thing at the correct time appears from the outside as a pool of serenity surrounded by a maelstrom of distraction. As the number and severity of distractions increase, we must rachet up focus/relaxation. When there are too many distractions, or an inappropriate focus, a "brainlock" occurs.

John Hamilton has identified four points when the brain locks up on a skydive. Difficulties first appear when trying to mentally review one step after another in an order. To break through this block he recommends skipping to the second or third step when mentally reviewing performance points.

After the exit, skydivers tend to do well up through the first or second performance point then lock up. Hamilton believes this happens due to focus lag on the exit. During exits, focus is often so concentrated that it takes a second or two to mentally move from being in the door to being in the air. By starting mental rehearsals at the second point it will be easier to pick up at the appropriate place once in the air.

Another brainlock point is catastrophic, or total brainlock. These are sometimes caused by practicing too fast. We can move from one performance point to the next only so fast, and no faster. To correct this problem drill performance points at a realistic speed. It is better to practice too slow than to practice too fast and trip up in the air. "There is nothing worse," reports Hamilton, "than when your body writes checks that your brain can't cash."

Finally, self confidence plays a large roll in brainlocking. Some skydives are simply more difficult to remember than others. Dive complexity can intimidate and trip one up into brainlocking over worrying about brainlocking. It's an easy trap to fall into.

One key to overcoming the confidence problem is to use positive reinforcers. Thinking, "Oh! I don't want to hit that tree," registers as, "Oh! I want to hit that tree." Saying to yourself, "I hope I won't forget the practice ripcord pulls this time," comes out as, "I hope I forget the practice ripcord pulls this time." It is difficult or impossible to visualize "not" doing. Try to not be conscious of your tongue right now. Hard to do isn't it?

It is more effective, and more reflective of a confident mental state, to express desires or goals in the positive. "Oh! I want to land in that clear area," and "I am doing practice ripcord pulls after my first circle of awareness," are instructions directing action and result in less brainlocking and more confidence. New activities, people and places generate varying degrees of stress. When evaluating stressors, understand that not all perceived threats are realistic. Non-skydivers, for example, often perceive that a parachute either opens or doesn't. If it opens, so goes the reasoning, the user is safe, and if it doesn't the user is doomed. Experienced skydivers know that there are degrees of parachute "openness" and understand that if deployment were interrupted that there are reasons for that blockage.

Environment can also induce perceptual distress. Simply being in freefall stresses some skydivers so much that they forget what they should do or when they should do it. Even the perception of failure or a threat to the ego can reduce performance.

Movement toward goals centers around controlling perception. The body moves toward the mind's most dominate thought. The secret to overcoming destructive thoughts is not through denial or avoidance, but in recognizing their existence and converting them to constructive expressions.

Skydiving guru Pat Works believes that all living things move at their own pace. Rivers, wind, dance, and skydives each ebb and flow with their own living rhythm. "All flow at their own rate," says Works. "You can never hurry up this rate of flow without disrupting it and getting out of sequence with your action. To ignore flow on the dance floor brings instant ridicule. To ignore flow is folly."

Flowing on a skydive, or being in the right place at the right time, depends on the selective application of awareness. And when stressors are reduced; when we clear away the fog of ignorance and laziness, we can more clearly see what should be the focus of our awareness and what should be allowed to pass without notice.

A Sonnet to Flow

Upon the early days of youth
There grew the vines of tasks undone,
While under the blue and vaporous booth
There lie the tools of life hard won;
We find a time to find the thing
That once within us dwelled:
The thing that lived but since took wing,
The thing that shrunk what once had swelled.
A rich and bright existence then
Which races ahead yet lags behind
Is the choice we're making when
We follow the choices of the blind.
Yet when we choose to follow flow
The early vines of youth still grow.

CONCLUSION

Awareness is a necessary part of everyday living. We should be aware of how much change we receive in restaurants. We must be aware of other cars relative to us on the freeway. We must be aware of what we are doing while we are doing it and how it will affect future events or risk taking action that is out of sync with our situation. Skydiving places increased demands on our awareness. It is this requirement for heightened awareness which attracts many to the sport. It is easy to immerse oneself completely in skydiving. But while so immersed we should develop a special sense of place and environment to keep ourselves out of trouble.

We can be killed or injured at any point during a skydive-- loading the airplane, riding to altitude, exit, in freefall, opening, landing, or walking off the landing area. Students: listen to your instructors and do what you are told while yearning to understand why. They are genuinely interested in your well-being and want to see you grow safely. Novices: ask lots of questions. Play what-if games with yourself and if you can't find a satisfactory answer ask someone you trust. Licensed skydivers: repeatedly practice those things you know you should be doing no matter how mundane you think they are or how well you think you know them. By practicing you develop adaptive habits and improve your level of awareness. You also teach by example whether you want to or not. Young skydivers constantly watch you for behavior cues. Be safe, be aware, stay alive to skydive another day.

Novice skydivers frequently want to try everything at once. Students get a license and want to be freestyle-relative work-camera flying-demonstration skydivers-- all on the same jump. Often their thirst for experience overrides their ability to realistically see the contents of their performance envelope.

Novice skydivers must first learn to operate the parachute. That means knowing inside and out, upside down and right side up the control, landing, and emergency procedures for the equipment used. Upon reaching the baseline the skydiver turns toward the wind line and "S" turns to bleed off excess altitude before facing the wind. At a height and angle that will bring the parachutist into the landing area, he or she turns to face the wind and prepares to land. A good indication of the landing pattern to use is the one used by other jumpers at similar experience and equipment levels. Watching what they did provides clues for successful approaches.

Extreme?

Why do this? Really. Why skydive? Some writers postulate that an "extreme" sport triggers a surge of gratifying (after it's over) hormones that pull a participant deeper and deeper into the activity. Others believe a system of social rewards keep edgeworkers coming back for more. "I've done it, you've done it, we know what the deal is. We're insiders." Still others report that a need for relief from the mundane; a drive to glimpse the tail of the curve; compels ordinary people to taste a little of the wild side where outcomes are uncertain.

There are dangers there to be sure. We have covered many herein. One danger not covered is the natural tendency of people to fall back on the familiar. It happens in skydiving just like it happens in other of life's arenas. First we get comfortable skydiving. Next thing we know we are mowing grass and packing parachutes for rides to altitude. Then we find ourself living in a hanger eating Ramen Noodles and trying to finagle a ride to the next boogie. Skydive, but keep life in perspective.

Looking to the opposite end of this spectrum we see workers trapped in cubicles for hours at a time. Little stimulation. No time for recreation (to be re-created). Skydiving offers this group an out. It gives Dilbert an opportunity to break out of that box. It provides incentive and opportunity to get in shape and keep the mind curious and creative. Skydiving can even give one back control and a sense of personal accountability.

Modern life has given us much. But it has taken some things away too. We are heaped with layers of responsibility. There are so many layers that personal responsibility has diluted to the point that we can almost always find someone else to point a finger at when life goes askew. Yet we are left with the desire to control; the desire to be personally responsible for ourselves. When you leave the door of an airplane it's all you.

Along with diluted responsibility we Americans are consumed by trivia. What matters? Is it having the new this or the improved that? Is it work? Spouse? Money? Skydiving can help one set priorities and see what is really within one's realm of control.

What makes an edgeworker sport is not the degree of risk to life and limb, but the degree that the activity taxes one's ability, talent, and skill. Skydiving challenges all three. It is one hell of a thrill too. As long as you know your limits, seek competent authority, accumulate technical skill, use the best equipment for the type of skydive, and maintain balance, you will enjoy a rich life at the drop zone for many years.

Learning and understanding are two different things. We can learn to pack without understanding what we are doing. We can learn to make a safe first jump without really understanding the subtlety, history and nuance; the flow behind what we are doing. To both learn to skydive and understand the skydive is sublime.

Questions for Thought

1. What two organizations direct skydiving's development in the United States?

2. How do you identify a properly open and functioning ram air parachute?

3. What action below do you take FIRST when confronted with a hazardous landing?

    a. Steer to avoid it
    b. Try to land on top of it
    c. Immediately turn 180 degrees
    d. Pull down on both steering toggles

4. How do you correct line twists?
    a. Perform emergency procedures
    b. Immediately release the steering toggles and attempt to turn toward the landing area
    c. Turn off the AAD and release the RSL
    d. Pull the risers apart and bicycle feet against the direction of the twists

5. At what altitude must you deploy a main parachute?

6. What is a decision altitude?

7. Which option below would be the best bail-out (emergency exit) procedure?
    a. Hold tightly to the instructor's cheststrap while he or she leaves the aircraft
    b. Jump out the door and pull the reserve ripcord handle
    c. Have both hands on the main or reserve handle before leaving the aircraft
    d. Confirm with the pilot that the aircraft is in trouble before moving to the door

8. What would you do if a pilot chute were released in the aircraft cabin?

     a. Give it to the instructor
     b. Try to contain it
     c. Toss it out the door
     d. Hold the pilot chute to the chest, and move as quickly as possible toward the rear of the aircraft

9. What are emergency procedures for an uncontrollable main parachute?

10. Which below describes the best landing under canopy?

     a. Hook the canopy on a tree to keep my feet off the ground
     b. Get my feet out in front of me and slide in on my butt
     c. Put my feet and knees together and roll along my side
     d. As I roll, stick my arm out to try to cushion my fall

11. When landing a round reserve parachute it is best to get a little downwind of the intended landing area. (True or False)

12. When landing a ram-air parachute it is best to get a little downwind of the intended landing area. (True or False)

13. Why is it important to learn to track straight and flat?

14. What could happen if one skydiver got below another skydiver in freefall?

15. Which groups exit the airplane first and why?

16. How does one check a pullout during an equipment check?

17. Why does it look like I am going to have a canopy collision as I land my parachute during a night jump?

18. What is the difference between flat and PRO packing?

19. In what situations could opening a parachute too high be dangerous?

20. Why do some jumpers flare at three feet while others flare at 12 to 15 feet?

21. What is the purpose of the slider?

22. What is the difference between Mean Sea Level and Above Ground Level? Why should it matter to skydivers?

23. Explain the function of each organization: FAI, NAA, PIA

24. What is the formula for calculating "wing loading"
   a. canopy surface/ exit weight
   b. cord/span
   c. exit weight/canopy surface
   d. porosity/jumper height

25. You have reached your deployment altitude and cannot find the main deployment handle. What do you do?
   a. Quickly develop a contingency plan
   b. Execute your preplanned contingency
   c. Wait for instructions from your instructor
   d. Continue to attempt locating the main deployment

26. You have reached your deployment altitude and cannot pull the main ripcord. What do you do?
   a. Attempt pulling the main handle a second time, then, if still unsuccessful, deploy the reserve
   b. Attempt pulling the main handle a second time, then, if still unsuccessful, cut away and deploy the reserve
   c. Pull on the main handle until the canopy deploys
   d. Attempt pulling the main handle a second time, then, if still unsuccessful, use the AAD

27. Cross your feet for a tree landing (T or F)

28. What was Domina Jalbert's contribution to skydiving?
    a. Conceived and developed the fabric airfoil
    b. Brought competition accuracy to the US
    c. Developed relative work skydiving in France
    d. Credited with first jumping a parachute

29. List three methods used to increase canopy speed for landing

30. What does FAR part 105 cover

31. What is the "span" of a ram air canopy

32. What is the proper packing sequence for a ram air parachute
    a. stow brakes, stow lines, flake nose, clear lines, bag canopy, close container
    b. stow brakes, bag canopy, stow lines, clear lines, flake nose, close container
    c. stow brakes, stow lines, clear lines, flake nose, bag canopy, close container
    d. stow brakes, clear lines, flake nose, bag canopy, stow lines, close container

33. Why would jumpers want to leave more time between exits on a windy day than on a calm day?

34. What would happen if the knees were lower than the pelvis in freefall?

35. Why is an ability to hold a heading necessary when skydiving with others?

36. Where is turbulence found?

REFERENCES

The Aerial Freestyle Guidebook by: Dale Stuart, softbound, 8.5X11 in., 72pp., $29.95 ill.
Written by a world champion freestylist, this work introduces the reader to 90 freestyle skydiving moves. She builds on this introduction to show combinations and transitions that can create an impressive series.

The Art of Freefall Relative Work by: Pat Works, softbound, 228pp., 8.5X5.5 in., $12.95 ill.
This is a classic text on both mechanical and spiritual relative work maneuvers. Basic body maneuvers, exits, swoops, docks, competition, and teaching are covered.

Basic Freestyle Notes by: Tamara Koyn, unbound, 30pp., 8.5X11 in., $14.95 ill.
The author discusses techniques and hazards for basic freestyle routines.

Body Pilot by: Carl Nelson, softbound, 8.5X11 in., 76pp. $8.95 ill.
An excellent source for learning relative work. Clear text complements excellent photography and illustrations.

Demo Details by: Brian Dormire, softbound, 160pp., 8.5X11 in. $22.95 ill.
Detailed instructions for planning an exhibition skydive, working with the FAA, forming a team, and dealing with unexpected surprises.

Flight Operations Handbook by: Ray Ferrell, softbound, 58pp., 8.5X11 in., $39.95
Covers pilot responsibilities- paperwork, coordination, weight and balance- when flying skydivers.

Flying the Camera: The Complete Guide to Freefall Photography by: Patrick Weldon, softbound, 112pp., 6X9 in. $24.95 ill. A basic, but practical guide to capturing images in the air.

High Performance Canopies by: John Chapman, Australian Parachute Federation, softbound, 8.5X11 in., 16pp. $4.95 Useful information for the modern, high performance canopy pilot.

Owning and Operating a DZ by: Dave Schulz, unbound, 189pp., 8.5X11 in., $25.00 Text offers solutions for organizing, opening, and running a parachute center.

Parachuting: The Skydiver's Handbook by: Dan Poynter, Parapublishing, softbound, 400pp., 5.5X8.5 in., $19.95 ill. By far the best selling work on the how-to of beginning skydiving.

Power Dive: Mental Muscle for Skydivers by: Dr. Melody Milam, Bobby Potter, and Erin Milam, softbound, 154pp., 8.5X11 in., $14.95 Step-by-step plan to help skydivers improve confidence and performance.

SKYDIVE by: Chris Donaldson, 128 pages, 2000, Trafalgar Square; illustrated, $29.95. Topics include: what to expect in your first jump course, how to fly a parachute, and advanced techniques.

Parachute Centers

Alabama

Alabama Skydiving Inc.
(205)884-6937

Emerald Coast Skydiving Center
(334)986-5618

Opelika Skydiving Association
(334)745-5529

Skydive Alabama
(256)736-5553

Skydive Headland
(334)791-3132

Alaska

Adventure Aviation Skydiving Center
(888)373-3699

Arizona

Arizona Airplay Skydiving
(520)627-8009

Desert Skydiving Center
(602)271-0440

Marana Skydiving Center
(888)647-5867

Skydive Arizona
(520)466-3753

Skydive Phoenix
(480)855-6555

Arkansas

Arkansas Aero-Sports
(501)327-0022

Central Arkansas Para Center
(501)834-2509

Skydive Skyranch
(888)456-JUMP

South Arkansas Skydivers
(870)231-6867

California

Adventure Center Skydiving
(800)FUN-JUMP

Bay Area Skydiving
(925)634-7575

California City Skydive Center
(800)2-JUMP-HI

California Parachute Club
(925)634-0575

High Desert Skydive
(760)373-2733

Jim Wallace Skydiving School
(800)795-3483

Madera Parachute
Center
(559)673-2688

Perris Valley Skydiving
School
(909)657-1664

Skydance Skydiving
(530)753-2651

Skydive California City
(888)373-4007

Skydive Elsinore
(909)245-9939

Skydive in Paradise
(530)872-3483

Skydive Lake Tahoe
(530)832-1474

Skydive Monterey Bay
(888)BAY-JUMP
Skydive Palm Springs
(760)345-8500

Skydive San Diego
(619)216-8416

Skydive San Francisco
(707)894-9241

Skydive Santa Barbara
(805)740-9099

Skydive Santa Rosa
(707)573-8116

Skydiving Adventures
(800)526-9682

Colorado

Denver Skydivers Inc.
(970)842-5000

Front Range Skydivers
(719)347-2035

Mile-Hi Skydiving
Center Inc.
(303)702-9911

Skydive the Rockies!
(719)265-9161

Connecticut

Boston-Hartford Skydive
Center
(860)774-5867

Connecticut Parachutists
Inc.
(860)871-0021

Delaware

Skydive Delmarva Inc.
(302)875-3540

Florida

Air Adventures of
Clewiston
(863)983-6151

Crestview Skydiving
Center
(850)682-4144

Freefall Adventures
(561)388-0550

Free Flight Skydiving
School
(352)748-6629

School of Human Flight
(850)627-SOHF

Skydive America Palm
Beach
(561)924-2020

Skydive City Inc.
(813)783-9399

Skydive Deland
(904)738-3539

Skydive Key West
(305)745-4FUN

Skydive Lake Wales
(863)678-1003

Skydive Miami
(305)SKY-DIVE

Skydive Naples
(888)447-5867

Skydive North Florida
(904)364-4358

Skydive Palatka
(904)328-0606

Skydive Sebastian
(800)399-JUMP

Skydive Space Center
(321)267-0016

Skydive Tampa Bay
(888)439-JUMP

Skydive University
(561)581-0100

Skydive Williston
(352)528-0012

Skyventure Wind Tunnel
(407)903-1150

Suncoast Skydiving
(941)923-7592

Williston Skydivers
(352)528-2994

Georgia
Atlanta Air Sportz
(706)234-3087

Atlanta Skydiving Center
(770)614-DIVE

Skydive Atlanta
(706)647-9701

Skydive Monroe
(770)207-9164

Hawaii
Air Tugie Production
Ltd.
(808)637-7007

Pacific International
(808)637-7472

Skydive Hawaii
(808)637-4121

Idaho

Skydive Idaho
(208)887-6042

Snake River Skydiving
(208)377-8111

Illinois

Archway Skydiving
Center
(800)283-JUMP

Chicagoland Skydiving
Center
(815)286-9200

Greater St. Louis
Parachute Club
(314)576-JUMP

Illinois Sky Sports
(217)893-1710

Illinois Valley Parachute
Club
(309)392-2751

Mid-America Sport
Parachute Club
(217)824-JUMP

Millennium Skydiving
(815)929-9000

Parachutes Over Carmi
(618)382-8921

Quad City Skydiving
Center
(309)944-0363

Skydive Chicago!
(815)433-0000

Skydive Illinois
(815)941-1149

Indiana

Aerodrome Sky Sports
(765)939-2939

America Skydiving
(219)962-1136

Jerry's Skydiving Circus
(812)988-4316

Jumpin' Indiana
(937)472-4050

Skydive Fort Wayne
(800)379-3340

Skydive Goshen
(219)493-1140

Skydive Indiana
(765)654-0300

Skydive Greensburg
(812)663-3483

Iowa

Accelerated Freefall
Iowa
(515)268-0403

Central Iowa Skydivers
(515)278-4261

Des Moines Skydivers
(515)243-1711

Paradise Skydives
(319)472-4975

Skydive Iowa
(515)282-1788

Kansas

Kansas State University
Parachute Club
(785)776-3639

Skydive Kansas
(913)RAD-DIVE

Skydive Suppesville
(316)682-3692

Skydive Wichita
(316)532-2828

Kentucky

Ft. Campbell Sport
Parachute Activity
(270)798-2737

Green County SPC
(502)348-9531

TKO Skydiving
(615)672-2855

Louisiana

Aero Resources
(888)YOU-JUMP

Ft. Polk Parachute
Activity
(337)531-5350

Skydive Acadiana
(337)276-3475

Maine

Central Maine Skydiving
(207)487-5638

Skydive New England
(207)339-1520

Maryland

Freefall Academy
(301)261-0188

Parachutes Are Fun
(800)232-9501

Skydiving Center at
Ocean City
(410)213-1319

Massachusetts

Airborne Adventures
Skydiving
(413)665-7577

Jumptown
(800)890-JUMP

Pepperell Skydiving
Center
(978)433-9222

Michigan

Central Michigan
Skydivers
(989)773-8858

Marine City Parahawk
(810)765-3242

Mid-Michigan Skydivers
(810)687-1398

Napoleon Skydiving
Center
(517)536-5252

Northern Exposure
Skydiving
(517)739-9006

Skydive Hastings
(877)867-5934

Skydive Michigan!
(616)781-9411

Skydive Tecumseh
(517)423-7720

Wild Wind Skydivers
(517)832-5780

Minnesota

Iron Range Skydivers
(218)744-3213

Minnesota Skydivers
Club
(952)431-1960

Skydive Hutchinson
(320)587-5875

SkyDive Twin Cities
(715)684-3416

Mississippi

Gold Coast Skydivers
(800)796-7117

Missouri

Freefall Express
(800)598-JUMP

Missouri River Valley
Skydivers
(800)SKY-DIVE

Quantum Leap Skydive
Center
(573)860-JUMP

Skydive Kansas City
(816)524-JUMP

Montana

Laurel Skydiving Center
(406)656-6897

Skydive Lost Prairie
(888)833-5867

Nebraska

Crete Skydiving Center
(402)488-5688

Lincoln Sport Parachute
Club
(402)333-2279

Nevada
> Las Vegas GravityZone
> (702)456-3802

New Jersey
> Skydive Cross Keys
> (856)629-7553
>
> Skydive Jersey Shore
> (732)938-9002
>
> Skydive Sussex
> (973)702-7000
>
> Sky's the Limit
> (973)940-6998

New Mexico
> New Mexico Air Adventures
> (505)797-2167
>
> Skydive New Mexico
> (505)797-2167

New York
> Finger Lakes Skydivers
> (607)869-5601
>
> Frontier Skydivers
> (716)751-6170
>
> Malone Parachute Club
> (518)497-6315
>
> Mohawk Valley Skydiving
> (518)370-JUMP

> The Ranch
> (845)255-9538
>
> Rochester Skydiving Center
> (716)589-9340
>
> Skydive Long Island
> (631)208-3900
>
> Skydive the Ranch
> (845)255-4033
>
> Verona SkyDiving Center
> (315)363-2763

North Carolina
> 82nd Freefall Activity
> (910)396-9989
>
> Carolina Sky Sports
> (919)496-2224
>
> Green Beret Sport Parachute Activity
> (910)907-2369
>
> Raeford Parachute Center
> (910)904-0000
>
> Skydive Coastal Carolinas
> (843)392-1479
>
> Skydiving Adventures
> (336)644-1737

Uof NC at Chapel Hill
(919)962-5546

U.S. Army Parachute
Team
(910)396-2036

North Dakota
Skydive Fargo!
(701)281-0149

Ohio

Aerohio Skydiving
Center
(330)925-5867

Alliance Sport Parachute
Club
(330)426-2565

Canton Air Sports
(330)823-0370

Taylor Air Sports
(740)687-1355

Tri-State Skydivers
(606)836-7475

Oklahoma
Oklahoma Skydiving
Center
(918)225-2222

Pegasus Skydiving
(405)222-1445

Skydive Hinton
(405)457-6500

Skydive Tulsa
(918)343-JUMP

Oregon
Eugene Skydivers
(541)895-3029

Skydive Oregon
(503)829-3483

Wright Brothers Skydiv-
ing
(541)461-5867

Pennsylvania
NEPA Ripcords
(570)788-2476

Chambersburg Skydiving
Center
(800)256-3497

Chuck Bryant's Skydive
Bouquet
(724)838-8861

Endless Mountain
Skydiving Club
(800)229-5557

Erie Skydivers
(814)899-6235

Maytown Sport Para-
chute Club
(717)653-0422

Pennsylvania Skydiving
University
(570)286-3172

Pittsburgh Skydiving
Center
(330)882-3871

Skydive Pennsylvania
(800)909-JUMP

The Skydivin' Place
(717)637-1866

United Parachute Club
(610)760-9010

Rhode Island

Boston-Providence
Skydiving Center
(401)333-3663

Skydive Newport
(401)845-0393

South Carolina

Blue Sky Adventures
(877)RIP-CORD

Flying Tigers SPC
(864)654-0840

Skydive Carolina!
(803)581-JUMP

Skydive Walterboro
(803)549-6660

Sumter Skydiving Center
(888)824-JUMP

South Dakota

Black Hills Air Sports
(800)794-5867

South Dakota Skydivers
(605)362-8204

Tennessee

Outlaws Skydiving
(931)232-5843

Skydive Paris
(901)642-4433

Skydive Smoky Mountains
(865)577-9798

Tennessee Skydiving
Center
(800)483-3483

Texas

Austin Skydiving Center
(979)773-9100

Eagle Flight Skydiving
(817)874-7591

East Texas Skydiving
Club
(903)SKY-DIVE

Galveston Island Skydiving Club
(281)648-2111

Ground Rush Skydiving
Club
(888)473-RUSH

Salado Skydive Center
(254)947-3483

Sky's the Limit
(361)358-9330

Skydive Dallas
(903)364-5103

Skydive Houston
(800)JUMP-OUT

Skydive San Marcos
(512)488-2214

Skydive Spaceland
(281)369-3337

Skydive Texas
(940)627-1100

SPI Skydivers
(956)761-6026

Westex SkySports
(915)683-JUMP

Utah

Ogden Skydiving Center
(801)627-JUMP

Skydive Salt Lake
(801)255-JUMP

Skydive Utah
(801)768-0999

Vermont

Vermont Skydiving
Adventures
(802)759-3483

Virginia

Adrenaline Air Sports
(540)296-1100

Hartwood Paracenter
(540)752-4784

Skydive Orange
(540)942-3871

Skydive the Point
(804)785-4007

Skydive Suffolk
(757)539-3531

Skydive Virginia!
(540)967-3997

West Point Skydiving
Adventures
(804)304-9954

Washington

Blue Skies Skydiving
Adventures
(253)588-1176

Kapowsin Air Sports
(360)893-3483

Skydive Snohomish
(360)568-1541

Skydive Toledo
(360)864-2230

West Plains Skydiving
Center
(509)245-3811

Wisconsin
AtmosphAir Skydiving
Center
(920)568-1700

Green Bay Skydivers
(920)822-5010

Seven Hills Skydivers
(608)244-5252

Sky Knight SPC
(800)38-CHUTE

Skydive Adventure
(920)685-5122

Skydive Superior
(715)392-8811

Skydive Wissota
Indianhead
(715)726-1616

Tri-State Skydivers
(608)723-6390

Wolf River Skydivers
(920)986-3212

U.S. Parachute Association
1440 Duke St.
Alexandria, VA 22314
(703)836-3495 ext. 301
fax: (703)836-2843
uspa.org

GLOSSARY

Accelerated Freefall - Instruction method using intensive supervision to accelerate learning.

Acceleration - A difference in speed from one point in time to another. Skydivers in freefall and not accelerating are said to have reached a terminal velocity

Accuracy - 1) A condition of being that is proximal to a target's center.
2) A skydiving sporting event in which participants attempt to land their parachutes as close as possible to a declared target.
3) Getting on the right airplane.

Arch - Fundamental freefall-stable body position.

Baglock - Parachute malfunction during which the parachute remains in the deployment bag.

Center float - Aircraft exit position outside the airplane and between the front and rear float positions.

Chunk - A freefall formation, or portion thereof, leaving the airplane en masse.

Coach - A specialist teaching the finer points of a specific skydiving discipline.

Count - The verbal, tactile, and visual cue used to synchronize a group exit.

Creepers - Horizontal training aids.

Currency - Number of jumps in a given period of time.

Demonstration - A skydive away from an established drop zone.

Diver - Aircraft exit position inside the door of the airplane.

Drop zone - Area suitable and used for sustained skydiving operations.

DZO- Drop zone operator (or owner).

Exhibition jump - Demonstration jump.

Exit transition - Movement through the forward throw of an airplane following exit.

FAA - Federal Aviation Administration

Freefall - Period after leaving the aircraft and before deploying an untethered parachute.

Front float - Aircraft exit position outside the airplane and most forward.

Heading - The direction faced or direction of movement.

Horseshoe - Parachute malfunction during which a part of the deploying parachute system snags on the parachutist or the parachutist's equipment.

Instructor Assisted Freefall - Similar to Accelerated Freefall, Instructor Assisted Freefall represents recognition of a combined-methods approach to skydive instruction.

Instructor Assisted Deployment - Instruction method in which initial student deployments are controlled by the instructor

Jump run - Period of level flight at jump altitude just prior to the exit.

License - Certificate recognizing general skill set mastery.

Malfunction - Parachute state representing an unacceptable rate of descent for landing.

Organizer - A specialist responsible for matching skydives to people and people to skydives.

Packer - A parachute rigger's apprentice.

Pitch - Nose high or nose low attitude relative to the horizon.

PLF - parachute landing fall

Presentation - The effectiveness with which one's center of gravity interacts with the relative wind immediately following exit.

Ram air parachute - An air-inflated, simi-rigid, wing-like structure.

Rating - Certificate recognizing mastery of specific skill sets.

Rear float - Aircraft exit position outside the airplane cabin and rearmost.

Relative work - Old term for Formation Skydiving.

Relative wind - The wind generated by, and relative to, a body in freefall.

Rigger - Rating issued by the FAA certifying the holder as authorized to inspect, maintain and pack the reserve parachute.

Roll - Side high or side low attitude relative to the horizon.

Skydive University - Formal post-graduate training program focusing on freefall and canopy flight.

Spinning malfunction - Parachute malfunction during which only part of the parachute is inflated and spinning around the uninflated part.

Spotting - Process of selecting and exiting over a ground reference point conducive to landing in the designated landing area.

Static line - A parachute tether, anchored to the airplane, and used to effect deployment.

Static Line Progression - Instruction method using static line deployment on the first jumps.

Steering lines - Lines attached to the trailing edge of a parachute and used for control of heading and speed.

Streamer - Parachute malfunction during which the parachute has cleared the deployment bag but no part has inflated.

Style - 1) A skydiving sporting event in which participants attempt to complete 360° turns and backloops for time. 2) How you look getting on the airplane.

Tandem - A parachute rig capable of carrying two people.

Tandem skydiving - Skydiving using tandem parachute technology.

Terminal velocity - A balance between the pull of gravity and the body's drag against the air.

Total malfunction - Parachute malfunction during which the deployment bag and risers remain stowed in the container after an attempted activation.

U.S. Parachute Association (USPA) - Association for skydivers.

Wind line - An imaginary line drawn in the direction the wind is blowing and running through the center of a landing area.

Yaw - Heading change from one point in time to another; usually expressed in degrees.

Zoo toggles - Specialty brake setting; usually used for fixed-object jumping.